SONGS

OF

DELIVERANCE

by
BILL BANKS

Power for Deliverance: Songs of Deliverance, by Bill Banks
ISBN # 0-89228-031-X

Copyright ©, 1987
   by Impact Books, Inc.
now **Impact Christian Books, Inc.**
332 Leffingwell, Suite 101,
Kirkwood, Mo. 63122

Cover Design: Mary Uhring

Scripture quotations are from the Authorized King James
Version, unless otherwise noted.

Printed in the United States of America

Foreword

Even though I have never met the author in person, I am first of all, amazed at how similar our thinking is on the subject of deliverance. The Spirit would seem to be leading us to the same conclusions.

I truly enjoyed the earlier work *Ministering to Abortion's Aftermath*. I found it to be an inspiring book, a must for those suffering in the wake of an abortion and for anyone who ministers to those so oppressed. The author's straightforward and unique teaching style, coupled with interesting testimonials, is highly instructive and his honesty in dealing with matters where we have yet to find final answers is most refreshing. The book is timely and readable. I strongly recommend it to all Christian workers, especially as its scope and importance goes considerably beyond the problem of abortion.

Songs of Deliverance is equally powerful in its impact, the many case histories effectively cut through any doubts a reader may have in regard to the ministry of deliverance. The revelation concerning Ephesians 6, was the highlight of the book for me, and I think nicely punctuates the testimonials, while leaving the reader with the thought of Jesus as our Deliverer uppermost in his or her mind.

Glenn G. Dudley, M.D.
Merrimac, Maine

Table of Contents

Introduction

I. God's Prophetic Theme for This Hour

Why has this book been written? This is an important question which every author and publisher should honestly face. I have recently felt the urging of the Lord to pass on to faithful men...

> "..Commit thou to faithful men, who shall be able to teach others also." (II Tim. 2:2b)
>
> "Iron sharpens iron; and one man sharpens another." (Prov. 27:17, RSV)

...some of the powerful revelations and deliverance techniques with which God has graced us. My desire is to make this available to others and to do it on a broader scale than I am able to do in person through speaking or teaching.

This book contains revelations which God has granted in individual cases, but they are truths that can be universally applied. Truth, if it is indeed truth, will be universally true at all times, in all places, for all individuals.[1]

I have discovered that these truths have just as much power to help those in need in England, in Haiti, in California, or in Pennsylvania as they do in St. Louis.

In a very real sense I stand in awe of the revelations in this book for I have seen them work! Also because I know I have not created them; I realize that I am merely a chronicler of these truths. I encourage you to partake of this material, receive and use what you find relevant to your

---

[1] Truth need not be relevant to be truth: truth can be truth without being relevant to a particular individual. For example, Jesus can forgive a murderer his sins; this is truth. Fortunately however, it isn't relevant truth for most of us. Thus relevancy doesn't affect truth, merely its usefulness to us.

situation or ministry, and to put the rest on hold until the Lord or need confirms it for you.

II. God's Timetable

Where are we on God's timetable? I believe this book is symptomatic of a current phase of a new aspect of a Move of God. The Lord is bringing forth a new prophetic, Scriptural theme for us in this end-time period. The former Scriptural theme in the preceding two decades has been Joel 2:28, as quoted by Peter in Acts 2:17, which very early became a rallying cry and theme of the Charismatic movement:

"And it shall come to pass in the last days, saith God, I will pour out of My Spirit upon all flesh."

God's *new theme* for this hour is to be found a few verses later in Joel 2:32 where He states,

"And it shall come to pass, whosoever shall call upon the name of the Lord shall be delivered."

The exact same *"whosoever"* is used in this passage as is used in the New Testament when it says, *"Whosoever* shall call upon the name of the Lord shall be saved." It's going to be just as easy to get delivered as it is to be saved. Deliverance is just as much a part of God's plan and program as is Salvation, and it's a vital part of His message for this hour *that Salvation and deliverance are available to whosoever is willing to receive.*

In the Sixties and early Seventies, God brought forth a new phase of his work with man, which has been variously referred to as the Charismatic Movement, the Neo [New]-Pentecostal, or the Renewal Movement. It has been a movement characterized by the restoration to the church of the long absent "Gifts of the Spirit" (healings, miracles, tongues, interpretations of tongues and the other gifts or "Spirituals" of I Corinthians 12:7ff) which had through the centuries been lost to man because of corruption, disuse,

2

misuse, and unbelief. The movement, although admittedly not without certain man-made flaws and excesses, has been perceived by most to be one fruited with joy and love.

However, in our day, the latter part of the 1980's, a new phase seems to have begun with an added dimension of emphasis upon the ministering of deliverance from all forms of bondage. The Lord has also placed in many hearts a cry that is echoed in and to be fulfilled in the promise of Joel's words, *"Whosoever shall call upon the name of the Lord shall be delivered!"*

The ministry of deliverance aspect of spiritual warfare isn't new; it has been going on throughout this era. But there is an heightened awareness of this form of ministry and a new depth of interest in it occurring throughout the world.

III. An Introduction to Deliverance Ministry

Let me start right off by stating a truth that may shock you. I find no Scriptural basis for a deliverance ministry. Permit me to clarify: Scripture is certainly clear that Jesus, our perfect pattern, spent much of His time ministering in the area of deliverance. Preaching, teaching, healing, and casting out spirits; He definitely spent more than one-fourth of His time dealing with demons, casting out demons, or involved with what would today loosely be called "the deliverance ministry."

He also clearly indicated the importance of deliverance in His own ministry. He did this in at least four ways: first at the beginning of His own ministry by quoting from Isaiah 61, stating that He had come to "heal the brokenhearted, *to preach deliverance* to the captives, and recovering of sight to the blind, to set at liberty them that are bruised." Next He stated that the sure proof of the coming of the Kingdom of God was the casting out of evil spirits [demons] by the *finger of God* which He equates with the Holy Spirit (Mt. 12:28).

3

> "But if I with the finger of God cast out devils, no doubt
> the kingdom of God is come upon you." (Lk. 11:20)

He also proved its importance by utilizing it so often. Most scholars acknowledge that at least one fourth of His ministry involved deliverance. Finally the extreme importance of deliverance intended by Jesus in His continuing ministry through His body, is indicated by His stating that the very first sign to follow them that believe would be *"in my name they shall cast out devils..."* (Mk. 16:17)

Nevertheless, deliverance should be only a part of a full fledged ministry which seeks to follow Jesus' pattern. It must be kept in balance along with healing, teaching, Salvation, baptism and evangelism: all working to create a perfectly whole person.

IV. Holy Anger!

I never wanted to be in the "deliverance" ministry. But almost from the very beginning of my deeper walk with the Lord, I found that I became furious with the devil when I saw God's people in bondage to him, being tormented and cowering in fear. It made me angry to see the perverse effect he was able to have upon God's people.

One of the first times that I experienced this anger was early in my new walk with the Lord. In the latter half of 1971, I was asked to be in charge of ministering to the needs for healing that came to the prayer room of a large weekly prayer meeting attended by about 300 people.

In one of the first sessions in the prayer room a young man with more zeal than experience, began trying to minister to a very meek, quiet boy who was more than six feet tall. The boy had obviously "blown his mind" with drugs: his pupils were dilated almost eclipsing the irises of his eyes, and his speech was slurred. Although he had visited the meetings previously, this was his first entry into the prayer room. The zealous individual may have been seeking to

4

impress the two "name ministers" who were visiting the prayer room. One was a man who ministered internationally and was celebrated for his "gift ministry" and had been our main speaker that evening, the other was a local evangelist who also ministered nationwide.

The zealous young man, who felt that he had been "called" to the "deliverance ministry" attempted to cast out a certain sexual spirit by name, which seemed to me totally inappropriate as there had been no indication of such a problem, except that the one ministering had been attempting to cast that same spirit out of several people in the preceding week. After a few minutes the demons in the boy apparently assessed the confusion in the situation and he began raging, cursing, and moving menacingly toward the zealot who rapidly retreated.

I looked to the two "name ministers" expecting to see these leaders take charge. However, I was instead surprised and shocked by what I saw. The local "name" minister was asking the visiting "big name" minister, whom I happened to know didn't believe in demons, "What do you make of all this?"

The "big name" minister's eyes were wide in fear, and all the color had drained out of his face. He could only mumble, "I dunno."

I felt real anger stirring at Satan for his audacity in daring to flaunt his puny power in the presence of God's people in a prayer room. I was even angrier at the powerless church, which could talk a good story, and profess great spiritual insight and discernment, but which, when confronted by one teenager with a few demons, cowered in fear. It was a disgusting situation, and I was angry!

Finally, I could take it no longer, and so I stepped into Satan's arena. I placed myself squarely in front of the demonized boy and said, "I rebuke you, Satan, and every demon manifesting in this boy. I bind these drug spirits and command them to come out of him in Jesus' name!"

The boy was tall! I'm six feet. Fully erect, I could look the boy squarely in the mouth. The boy, who'd been a high school football star, hauled back his right arm, and launched his clenched fist directly for my face. I stood my ground, figuring that it was better to be bloodied if necessary in the Lord's service than to be ruled by fear as the rest were. His fist stopped about four inches from my face as if it had hit an invisible shield.

I was both relieved and blessed, because this confirmed for me that I was on the right track and that heaven was on my side. The demons and the boy apparently came to the same conclusion and he began to back away from me. (I noticed at this point out of the corner of my eye, that the 'name ministers' were taking this as their opportunity to flee.)

I continued the spiritual attack, commanding the drug spirits to come out. The shoe was on the other foot now. Finally the retreating boy reached the wall of the prayer room, and began trying to climb it. Looking back over his shoulder at me, fear evident in his face, he whined, "I believe in demons, now! I believe in demons!"

The boy received a small measure of help that night, but his problems were severe. We later learned that he had been an "A" student, graduating with honors, scholarships and (his version of the story was) that while in college at a party someone had slipped something into the punch (probably LSD or PCP) and it had "blown his mind."

He has received numerous miraculous touches from the Lord over the years, when he has been willing to seek help. Once he came to our meeting seeking prayer for his sight, unable to see well enough to read. After the Lord touched him, he was able to read the fine print on the back of a credit card at arm's length; a feat most of the people present couldn't equal with their glasses on. Today he has a job, although he needs further help.

* * * * * * *

6

The accounts which follow are not recorded to exalt any man, any institution, nor any particular method(s) of ministry...they point rather, as all testimonies should, to the glory of God, and should, if properly understood, cause joy in the hearts of believers, hunger in the hearts of those who have not come to know Him in His fullness, and produce the Scriptural result of the ministry of Jesus...."the people all glorified God, saying we never saw it on this fashion before."

They are also presented with the hope that believers may be better "equipped," through the understanding that will be imparted through the hearing of these accounts ... "for the work of the ministry."

Two keys that I trust will be found in this book are balance and flexibility, both of which really boil down to truly relying upon the Word of God for Truth and the Holy Spirit for Guidance. When this is done in faith, the captives will soon be singing *"songs of deliverance."* (Ps.32:7b)

PART ONE

Problems May Enter
Early in Life

Songs of Deliverance

"Thou art my hiding place; thou shalt preserve me from trouble: thou shalt compass me about with songs of deliverance." (Ps. 32:7)

Case 1   Deliverance Defeats Suicide

One night about 10:00 after a particularly tiring day, my wife and I were just preparing to turn out the lights when the phone rang. It was a good friend, a young Spirit-Baptized woman of about 26 whom we hadn't seen for nearly a year since she and her husband had moved to an outlying community.

Her voice was trembling and I could tell that she'd been crying, as she said, "I have to see you right away! I know that I need deliverance! I'm desperate!"

Having in the past received similar nighttime calls from distraught people, I started probing to determine whether the situation was really as desperate as she thought. "What makes you think that you have a demon?" I asked.

She blurted out tearfully, "I hate to bother you so late at night, but I *know* that I have a *spirit of suicide* — because I decided to kill myself this evening on the way home from choir practice by driving off the Second Street bridge; but God prevented me from killing myself."

She paused for a breath and I asked dubiously, "How did *God prevent you* from killing yourself?"

Matter-of-factly she replied, "He had a nine year old boy ask me to give him a ride home, and I just couldn't let him be hurt. No one had ever before asked me for a ride in ten years in the choir. I really need help!"

11

I invited her to come on over...realizing in my spirit that God had definitely arranged for her to be able to get ministry...not only because He'd spared her life, but also because our evening was free. Even though we were already exhausted, I knew we had to help her if we could. His grace and strength had recharged us by the time she arrived.

As we began to minister to Charity[1], I quickly reviewed mentally all the details I could recall of her situation: she and her husband were active members of a large Methodist church, both sang in its choir; although she had received the Baptism in the Holy Spirit about two years previously and had entered into a deeper walk with the Lord, she had been out of fellowship with like minded believers since moving; I was also aware that her husband had been having an affair with another woman, and had been hinting at the possibility of a divorce for quite awhile. One of their major problems had been their inability to have children. Although the picture was rather grim, none of these conditions was recent nor likely to have triggered this response.

Charity interrupted my reflections, "I have no idea what set me off tonight, nor why I should suddenly become suicidal; but I definitely wanted to end it all, and would have, if Jimmie hadn't asked for the ride. My marriage situation is deteriorating, but he still doesn't seem to be in any hurry to do anything. It's all just so.... empty."

After we had begun to pray with Charity, had asked the Lord to guide us and to reveal the source of her problem, she suddenly exclaimed, "I just saw something that I don't understand at all. I saw in my mind's eye a house that I lived in before I was age five." She went on embarrassedly, "I don't know how to talk about this because it's embarrassing and it involves my parents."

I reminded her that her life was more important than

---

[1]The names and identifying facts throughout this book have been changed to protect the privacy of the individuals. The cases are otherwise factual.

her pride, or her parents' reputation. Her life was literally at stake.

Seemingly reassured, she continued, "My parents always had pornography lying around in that house, but after we moved into our new home, just before I turned five, I never saw it again. I guess they thought then I was too old to be allowed to see it." She explained.

Since the Lord had apparently brought this to her mind, I decided to pursue it and commanded the *spirit of Pornography* to manifest itself and to come out of her. I was also led to do something I don't ever recall doing prior to that occasion, I also commanded every spirit related to pornography to come out as well. (I must admit that at that point in time, I wasn't even sure that there was such a thing as a *spirit of Pornography*, although it seemed logical that there could be.)

Eight spirits then named themselves and we commanded each out in turn: the first was *pornography*, the next *foolishness*[2] and then *harlotry*. This dear, sweet girl was clean cut, soft spoken, gentle and refined. However, one thing that had always seemed out of place was her clothing. She always appeared to be dressed suggestively, in sweaters that were too small, or blouses cut too low, and skirts or slacks that were too tight.

I suddenly realized the obvious in light of what we were discovering in the spiritual realm, she had been dressing like a pin-up, or similar to the pornographic pictures which she'd seen in her childhood (and which she probably thought her parents, or at least her father, admired). In previous ministry I had counselled with Charity concerning her "suggestive" clothing as being inappropriate for certain functions, and as being out of character with both her character and her witness. She had explained it away as being "the way her husband wanted her to dress," citing examples where he had even gone shopping with her and picked

---

[2] I later found a Scriptural confirmation which could account for such a spirit, "Foolishness is bound in the heart of a child." (Pr. 22:15)

out some of her clothing. (Probably indicative of problems on his part.)

Each spirit was commanded to leave as soon as its presence (name) was revealed. I was dumbfounded when I addressed the seventh spirit, "you next spirit name yourself and come out of her," and heard it respond with a whine... "I am the spirit of *STERILITY*." I was shocked because I had never dreamt that sterility could be a spirit, having always considered it a purely physical condition. The shock was also a pleasant one, in the sense that it could so logically explain why they had been incapable of having children.

Although at first I was somewhat concerned that some other spirit might be lying to us, I sternly commanded *sterility* to leave and it did. Then *suicide* named itself and was cast out. She began to laugh...she was free!

I told her as she left, that for me, the proof of deliverance was not whether or not the person coughed, gagged, belched, yawned or manifested some other symptom: the proof of deliverance is *whether the person can walk in freedom*. "The real proof of the validity of your deliverance from *sterility* will be when you have your first child. Please send me a picture when you have that first baby."

I wish the story could end with a happy ending right at this point, but it didn't. Charity went home rejoicing, eager to tell her husband about her deliverance, new-found freedom, and the possibility that their childlessness had been potentially cured. However, when she arrived home, her husband told her he didn't want to hear anything she had to say, that he definitely wanted the divorce, and he walked out. Several months later, in spite of her efforts to prevent it, the divorce went through.

> **IMPORTANT TRUTH:**
> For me the fruit of deliverance is whether or not
> freedom from bondage occurs...

For me the fruit of deliverance is whether or not freedom from bondage occurs...just as the fruit of healing is the loss of pain or symptoms. I had shared this thought with Charity that night after her deliverance, and told her that I knew God had done a mighty work in her, but only He could confirm the validity of the deliverance or healing which had taken place. I then asked her to be sure to let me know when the baby arrived. She promised to do so.

Two years or more after her divorce, Charity remarried to a fine young man, and within a year and a half their first child was born. True to her word, Charity called me from the hospital the morning after her child was born to praise the Lord for His goodness and power, and to thank us for praying with her. She then sent a picture of a beautiful child. I have since received three more pictures from her, as God has abundantly confirmed His ministry to her.

Insights / Giving Understanding: ABIMELECH'S CURSE

The twentieth chapter of Genesis contains a Scriptural principle which has bearing upon this case.

> "So Abraham prayed unto God: and God healed Abimelech, and his wife, and his maidservants; and they bare children.
> "For the Lord had fast closed up all the wombs of the house of Abimelech, because of Sarah Abraham's wife."
> (Gen. 20:17-18)

We can see in this passage, a truth and a spiritual principle that God would not have us miss. A truth that has been reiterated and a principle that has been repeatedly confirmed as I have shared these truths across the country.

Because of sexual immorality (Abimelech took Sarah into his harem with the obvious intention of having sexual relations with her. The sin in this case was *intended adultery* even though Abimelech wasn't aware of it. God revealed the danger to him in a dream.) A righteous curse (a curse from God for breaking, albeit potentially, one of His commandments) was incurred. The nature of the curse was *childlessness*. (He caused a stopping of the wombs) that was brought upon the entire household of Abimelech from his wife to his maidservants. It's a blessing to note in the Genesis account, that God's goal was *restoration to righteousness*. In this account can also be seen, that God's loving motivation was to save all the parties involved.

When the sin was recognized as sin (being exposed by God to Abimelech in the dream), repented of, and forgiveness, or restoration with God sought, then healing resulted. (The curse was lifted.)

Clearly in this case from Scripture — *childlessness* was a *curse* resulting from sin (a specific sin, of a man looking upon a woman with sexual desires, then lusting, desiring her as a sexual partner even though he did not have a proper basis for such a relationship with her, through marriage. The action of sin associated with pornography is essentially the same — looking with lustful desire upon a picture of a woman (usually scantily clad or unclad) with the goal of deriving sexual pleasure from the act of looking.

OBSERVATIONS:

On numerous occasions around the country while teaching or ministering in the area of healing, couples have come seeking prayer for the problem of childlessness. In those situations when I've been led to share Charity's story with them, most have responded that they identified with her situation, had themselves either been victims of, or had themselves sinned with pornography, and requested prayer to break all ties with the sin of pornography, and to have the curse broken and the spirit cast out.[3]

Incidentally, we were never able to learn what triggered the spirit of suicide in Charity at church that evening. Something caused the spirit to surface. My theory is that she probably saw something that reminded her of the pornography. It wasn't a conscious recollection, but stirred the spirit within her. Perhaps something as unlikely as another lady in the choir sitting in a particular position or looking similar to someone whom she had seen in one of the pictures from her childhood. In any event "...we know that all things work together for good to them that love God, to them who are the called according to His purpose," and God wanted Charity free!

*** REVELATION: ***
STERILITY WAS A SPIRIT IN THIS CASE.

*** REVELATION: ***
THE *SPIRIT OF PORNOGRAPHY* WAS RECEIVED
AS EARLY AS AGE 5, OR BEFORE.

*** REVELATION: ***
PORNOGRAPHY WAS A DANGEROUS
DOOR OPENER.

*** REVELATION: ***
A BEAUTIFUL SPIRIT-FILLED YOUNG WOMAN
HAD SPIRITS WHICH NEARLY DESTROYED HER
LIFE.

---

[3]For additional information concerning possible spiritual causes of childlessness, see the book *Ministering to Abortion's Aftermath,* and a forthcoming book, in this series, *Power for Deliverance From Childlessness.*

Less than a year later the Lord used the case of Sally and "IT" to reconfirm some of these issues and to reveal still more truth which He had in store for us.

Case 2   Deliverance for Sally From "IT"

Sally, a young nurse from our fellowship phoned one day to ask if my wife and I would pray with her.

"I know that I need some further deliverance. I don't have any idea what it is that I'm up against this time, but I'm sure it isn't *rejection* because we've already dealt with that and I really believe that it is gone. This is something that is similar to rejection though," she said thoughtfully.

"I know that I'm saved and that the Lord loves me, and that I've been baptised in the Spirit and walking with Him, for over five years but there is still something tormenting me."

I reflected upon the previous ministry with Sally. She had been adopted when only a few days old by an older couple who had lovingly raised her. Having been raised in a home as an only child, by older parents and knowing that she'd been adopted, Sally had experienced some *rejection* and *abandonment* problems. She had been delivered of both spirits about six months earlier and had also forgiven her 'birth-mother' for abandoning her.

"It's embarrassing to talk about, but I'm sure most girls, or women think of themselves as female; as a 'she' or a 'her,' but for some reason, I always think of myself as an 'it.' I really don't understand it, but that's always been the way that I've thought of myself. And besides, I'm almost thirty years old, and all the dates I've had in my life you could count on one hand. I'm not upset about it because I've had no desire to date either."

I recalled that we had always known Sally to be a friend-ly outgoing, loving, patient, and compassionate Christian. We had observed that although she was very pleasant and everyone liked her, she did not date. In spite of the fact that

18

she had a great personality, Sally seemed to have no desire to date and did not seem, upon reflection, to be particularly feminine. She always dressed neatly but not in a very feminine way, almost like a tomboy, usually wearing the typical pantsuit outfit nurses wear, and she wore her hair close-cropped.

It was certainly an odd symptom, and certainly sounded abnormal, unnatural, and probably demonic. However, being totally in the dark as to what we were up against, I suggested that we just pray and ask God to intervene. So we simply prayed something to this effect, "Lord Jesus, we acknowledge that you are the Deliverer. It is your ministry and we know that you know all about Sally's problems and you want her whole even more than we do. In Your name we command this thing tormenting her to identify itself and to come out of her."

Then we just waited...

Sally began to shake and shiver. It was evident to us that the Lord was doing something and that she was apparently seeing something... therefore we decided to simply wait and let the Lord finish His sovereign ministry to her. A few minutes later she looked up, her eyes wet with tears, and said, "Wow! You won't believe what the Lord just showed me. I was in a large white room and I began to be able to see details. You know I'm a nurse, so I instantly recognized the scene as a hospital delivery room. I could see the clock on the wall. I could see the delivery room staff milling around. I could hear everything they said. I knew everything going on in that room. It was amazing to me, and then I noticed that there was a woman on the table who had obviously just given birth."

Sally paused briefly for a breath and continued her description of what she'd seen, "And, suddenly, I felt myself being carried from the corner where I was, out toward the center of the room, and I realized with a start, that *I was the new-born baby!* The nurse carrying me, attempted to

19

hand me to the new mother. She took one look at me with a sneer on her face, put up a hand to stop the nurse and snarled, "Get *IT* out of here!"

She sighed deeply and we all then realized that the curse of being an "it" had, in essence, been laid upon her from the moment of her birth. As a result of her being unwanted by her mother and put up for adoption she had not only picked up the *spirit of Rejection*, and the *Spirit of Abandonment* from which she had previously been delivered, but this unusual and peculiar spirit which had caused her to think of herself as an 'it.' We then prayed again with her, breaking the curse of being an 'it' and cast out the spirit which made her think of herself as 'it.' This peculiar rejection spirit was no doubt a member of the self-rejection family.

After she was delivered, Sally asked that we pray with her that she might be able to start dating, "preferably a Spirit-filled man." Within a week she was back to say "You won't believe this. I can scarcely believe it, myself, but the Lord has answered that prayer. Would you believe, I have been dating a Spirit filled man, and he has asked me to marry him!" As it turned out, Sally didn't marry him, but it blessed us all to see how far 'beyond our ability to think or ask' the Lord could do.

*** REVELATION: ***
AN INDIVIDUAL CAN RECEIVE A SPIRIT FROM THE MOMENT OF BIRTH.

*** REVELATION: ***
A SPIRIT PICKED UP IN CHILDHOOD OR IN-FANCY CAN HAVE A SERIOUS EFFECT EVEN ON THE LIFE OF A SPIRIT-BAPTISED BELIEVER.

> ***** REVELATION: *****
> SOMETIMES THERE ARE INDICATIONS IN THE
> PERSONALITY OR LIFE-STYLE OF THE INDI-
> VIDUAL THAT GIVE CLUES AS TO THE SPIRITS
> INVOLVED.

The Lord was about to expand our understanding by revealing an amazing truth concerning an unusual eating disorder....

Case 3   First Encounter With the Spirit of the Fear of Starvation

One evening a young minister came for deliverance accompanied by his wife. After he'd received deliverance, his wife said almost sheepishly, "Mr. Banks, I feel that I need some deliverance too."

I asked my standard question, "Mary, what makes you think that you have a demon?"

"I need deliverance from a *spirit of gluttony.*"

"You've got to be kidding." I exclaimed taken by surprise. But it was a natural reaction, Mary was what I would describe as being on the thin side of normal.

She then explained, "I know I'm not heavy now and don't look like it, but it's true, Mr. Banks. I am fine until Spring rolls around, and I begin to think about getting into a swimming suit. You see I work as a secretary to supplement Jim's income, and I put weight on around my thighs. I am fine until Spring rolls around," she repeated, "and then I begin thinking about putting on a swimming suit. The moment I make the decision to diet to take off the unwanted weight, *something in me just goes nuts!* I will go to the refrigerator and eat everything in it. I will eat until I become physically sick." Mary slumped back into her chair, tears filling her eyes. "I really want help." she said

21

plaintively.

As she was speaking, the Lord had revealed to me (perhaps through a gift of knowledge — I don't know how to explain it, other than, that suddenly I knew) that her problem was a *spirit of the fear of starvation* which she'd had from infancy! I asked, "What do you know about the early part of your life?"

Mary seemed a little startled but then smiled, and said, "It's funny you should ask, because the only thing I know is that my mother told me recently I cried for the first two weeks I was alive."

"Why did you cry for those two weeks," I inquired following up on what I felt sure was a leading from the Lord.

"Because at the end of those two weeks the doctors discovered that my mother had an insufficient milk supply. They then gave me a supplemental bottle of formula, and from that time on I was fine," Mary explained.

She had picked up the spirit of *the fear of starvation* as a newborn. It never bothered her, never manifested itself, *until* she cut off the food supply. When the food supply was jeopardized, this 'thing' in her went beserk just as it did in her as an infant, and she would eat everything she could get her hands on.

Mary was, incidentally, a Born-again, Spirit-baptized Christian prior to the time she came for help. Shortly afterwards she and her husband left the St. Louis area to minister in the northern United States.

*** REVELATION: ***

SYMPTOMS CAN BE CONFUSING: MANIFESTATIONS MAY SOMETIMES BE THE OPPOSITE OF WHAT WE'D EXPECT.

```
*** REVELATION: ***
SPIRIT ACQUIRED IN FIRST DAYS OF LIFE,
ONLY APPEARED WHEN FOOD SUPPLY JEOP-
ARDIZED. WOMAN WAS ABLE TO FUNCTION
NORMALLY EXCEPT WHEN THE SPIRIT WAS
STIRRED UP.
```

```
*** REVELATION: ***
SUBJECT EXPERIENCED GUILT AND SHAME
OVER THE BEHAVIOR MANIFESTED WHILE THE
EVIL SPIRIT WAS ACTIVE, ADDING TO HER
TORMENT.
```

OBSERVATIONS:

Mary logically assumed that her problem was gluttony when in truth it was the opposite, the *fear of starving*. Evil spirits often don't manifest unless something triggers them. They may remain latent and hidden for years, until a stimulus is provided that provokes or stirs them up. When they surface, or their symptoms become evident they should be dealt with as soon as practicable, as the Lord has allowed their presence to be discerned.

God invites us to test and try Him in Malachi 3:10 with regard to financial matters. I believe that He also desires for us to prove Him of His faithfulness in other areas by daring to ask Him to do the things which He has promised to do, such as to heal in answer to prayer (James 5:15, Mk. 16:18), and to deliver people (Mk. 16:17, Mt.10:1). I was encouraged by Mary's deliverance from the *spirit of the fear of starvation,* to try ministering deliverance to myself.

The night following Mary's deliverance, a thought occurred to me and I shared it with my wife just before turning out the lights in our bedroom. "You know, in view of what we saw with Mary last night, I probably have a *spirit of colic*, because my parents told me that I cried with colic the whole year that I was two. If I ever had that spirit, I must still have it because no one would have thought of casting it out. I'm going to treat it as a spirit and command it to leave. Agree with me."

I then commanded the *spirit of colic* to come out of me. I had no preconceived expectations whatsoever. However, instantly I experienced a sensation as if someone had lit a match in my lower intestines. As I continued to command the thing to come out, I could feel it moving up through my intestines as if it were a puff of hot smoke. When it got to the area of my lung it was gone.

I would never have believed that such a thing were possible until it was confirmed to me. In thinking back, I had been troubled in college with frequent stomach pain which they thought was a duodenal ulcer. On one occasion they had me on an operating table ready to remove my appendix until the blood tests came back indicating that I didn't need it removed. So there was a history of stomach trouble which may have been a result of its presence.

Again we see a principle: that when God moves supernaturally, *it often builds faith and stimulates others to seek blessings at His hand.*

TEACHING SECTION I

Good news! God has made provision to set people free from every type of bondage.

I. **Ministry of Deliverance Is Available**
- A. **What Is Deliverance?**
- B. **Splinter-Deliverance**
- C. **What Are Demons?**
- D. **What Are the Goals of Demons?**
- E. **How Can Christians Have Demons?**
- F. **Primary Focus of All Ministry Must Be Jesus**

I. MINISTRY OF DELIVERANCE IS AVAILABLE

A. What Is Deliverance?

There is a valid place for the ministry of deliverance in the body of Christ today. It has been truthfully stated, "You cannot deliver the flesh": and by the same token, one cannot crucify a demon! *The flesh must be crucified and demons must be cast out!*

Deliverance is, of course, the casting out of evil spirits or demons, a subject which seems very foreign to us in our modern, sophisticated society, yet it was an area of ministry in which Jesus engaged. At least one fourth of his earthly ministry was devoted to dealing with demonic problems and the casting out of demons. Jesus cast out *spirits of infirmity* (Lk. 13:11), *of blindness* (Mt. 12:22), *spirits causing speech problems* (Lk. 11:14), *causing torment* (Mt. 15:22), *causing aberrational behavior* (Lk. 8:27), and causing *suicidal behavior* (Mk. 9:22) to mention but a few. This deliverance ministry wasn't limited to Jesus alone, but was rather something He commissioned those who followed Him to also make available (Mk. 16:17, Mt. 10:8).

We do, indeed, find the followers of Jesus engaging in this ministry of deliverance as the ministry of the "pattern evangelist" Philip bears testimony. We can observe his ministry in Samaria (Acts 8:7) where "unclean spirits crying with loud voice, came out of many that were possessed with them." Paul also ministered deliverance from an occult *spirit of divination* to a young girl who was following him and Silas (Acts 16:18).

Deliverance is largely a matter of cause and effect, or actually the reverse, *noting effect and seeking the cause*. Deliverance is often very logical and methodical detective work. It is, as stated, largely a matter of finding out what the source, cause, or root of the problem manifesting is, and then casting it out.

B. Splinter — Deliverance

We look for a splinter under the surface of the [...] one experiences splinter-like pricking pain. Ju[...] looks for the thing(s) that has caused the manife[...] discomfort, harassment, torment, or fear. One ha[...] tions with regard to splinters, to take the analogy a step further. One could put a bandage over the entry hole, and the skin would heal over the splinter. However, this is an unsatisfactory solution, because every time the spot is touched, it still hurts. The source of the pain is still there.

The second, and preferable alternative, is to undergo the momentary discomfort and perhaps even pain, of facing the splinter, and digging it out, so that the healing can be complete.

The same thing holds true in deliverance. It is preferable to undergo the momentary discomfort, embarrassment, or even pain to be able to be freed from the source of the problem.

C. What Are Demons?

A demon is an evil spirit; a spirit which is almost the exact opposite of an angel. An angel is a good entity, designed and directed by God to aid and bless mankind, who works for man's good. A demon, on the other hand, operates under the direction and control of Satan, the "prince of devils," and is an evil entity. The spirit's goal is to harass, torment, frustrate, and generally make life miserable for man.

Demons are disembodied spirits. They desire to have bodies through which to manifest their own lustful natures. The *demon of rejection,* as an example cannot be rejected until it is able to inhabit a human body which might be able to feel (experience) rejection. Often spirits work hand in hand with other spirits to accomplish their goals. The *rejection spirit would often tend to work in conjunction with a rejection-causing spirit.* The *spirit of rejection* lusts to be rejected by someone, lust cannot be fulfilled or satisfied until it is actually rejected. Therefore its cohort spirit must do something to cause the individual within whom it dwells to be rejected.

As an example, let's assume that I have a *spirit of rejection*. I might look at you and notice that you are wearing a blue jacket and a green shirt. The *rejection causing spirit* might prompt me to tactlessly say, ''Those colors look terrible on you,'' ''You shouldn't wear green with your complexion.'' Or ''You shouldn't have worn a blue jacket with that shade of green.'' Whatever I actually said really wouldn't matter, and even if you didn't dignify my comment with a response, the *spirit of rejection* could still torment me with something like, ''Did you see that look in those eyes? She really hates you! Boy, she thinks that you are as big a jerk as I've been telling you that you are.'' The effect is what these spirits working in tandem desire, to produce rejection, hurt and torment. It is not uncommon for the person who experiences compulsive feelings of rejection to himself become compulsively critical and fearful of others.

D. What Are the Goals of Demons?

Demons have something more important to do than merely make one feel miserable, although they spend a good deal of time and effort in this category of activity. The primary battle plan assigned to them by their commander-in-chief, Satan, is apparently threefold. Their first and primary goal is to prevent a person from accepting Jesus as Lord and Saviour. Failing to accomplish the primary goal, the secondary goal is to prevent the believer from serving Jesus at all, if possible, or at the least to minimize the person's effectiveness as a believer. They attempt to prevent him serving up to his potential. Thirdly, if the former goals have been unattainable, the demons attempt to cause the believer to turn away from God: to deny Jesus, to get to a point of serving Satan, or if possible, to destroy himself. It is certainly unpleasant to think that we have an enemy who is so ruthless, and so dedicated to our destruction, but we do!

Therefore, *we must not be ignorant of the wiles of the enemy*, and should prepare ourselves fully for spiritual warfare.

E. How Can Christians Have Demons?

Rarely a week goes by that I don't hear the questions, "How is it possible for me as a Christian to have this demonic problem?" or "How can I as a Christian have a demon?"[1]

The first thing Christians and especially candidates for deliverance should understand is that although the King James consistently translates as "possessed" the Greek word, *daimonizomai*, it's true meaning is *to have a demon*, or *to be (vexed) with a demon*.[2] Clearly a Christian cannot be "possessed" in the sense of exclusive ownership by both God and Satan. The Christian has clearly been purchased by, and *belongs to, Christ*.

Let me share four illustrations which have often been of help us in grasping truths about deliverance. They are only necessary because the world's view of demons has become so entrenched within Christian thinking.

1. Jesus Fulfills Many Roles

A crippled person might come into a meeting today, meet Jesus as Healer and be totally healed. However, his having validly met Jesus as Healer doesn't mean that he has met Him as Saviour. Similarly, to have met Jesus as Saviour doesn't automatically assure that he has also met Him as the One who "baptises with the Holy Ghost," or as the Deliverer. In His various ministries to us, Jesus fulfills a number of different roles, but it is incumbent upon us to seek Him for the blessing desired.

---

[1]Many more insights on this issue will be presented in a subsequent volume.

[2]James Strong, *Strong's Exhaustive Concordance* (Grand Rapids, Mich: Baker Book House, 1978). Greek Dictionary –1139. Eleven times in the New Testament when referring to possession or being "possessed," this word is used.

2. A Cold

When you have a cold, the cold doesn't have you; you have the cold. Your logical goal is to get rid of it.

3. "Under the Influence of Alcohol"

We, as Christians, have free-will: we can still choose to sin. We may, for example, go to the local pub and take a drink. If we continue to drink, our being Christians, will not protect us from becoming drunk. Frequently we hear or read accounts of moral, upright people having too much to drink and doing things they would never have even considered doing while sober.

Thus, it is clear that our being saved or even "Spirit-filled," does not prevent our coming *under the influence of alcohol*. Demons do not own us, but they can "influence us," by adversely affecting our attitudes, our behaviour, our thought lives, our spiritual growth, our vocabulary, our morals, our mannerisms, or our appetites. When present, they can condemn, harass, torment, or vex us causing obsessions, addictions, compulsions, fears, and in extreme cases self destructive or even suicidal behaviour.

Many Christians have already spent far too much time and effort attempting to pinpoint theologically the location of demons. "Are they within, or without?" "Do they 'possess' (obviously no!), obsess, oppress?" All these issues are largely irrelevant to the one being influenced or tormented by a demon.

4. The Knife Blade

If I have a knife blade sticking into my stomach, it really matters little to me whether the handle of the knife is on the inside or the outside: what I desire is to have the blade removed from my flesh!

To summarize: there is no such thing in Scripture as "demon possession." The goal of any Christian who feels that he is being compelled, coerced, harassed, or otherwise tormented by an evil spirit should be to immediately seek deliverance.

F. Primary Focus of All Ministry Must Be Jesus

It cannot be over emphasized that the PRIMARY OBJECTIVE of the one ministering is to be certain that the candidate for deliverance KNOWS JESUS, and if not, the number one GOAL of ministry must be to rectify that problem.[3]

Approximately one-third of the individuals who have come to us over the last seventeen years seeking deliverance, have had their needs met when they either accepted Jesus as Saviour, or as the Baptizer in the Holy Spirit. What they had assumed to be a need for deliverance was, in actuality, a need for Salvation or the Baptism in the Holy Spirit.

Although not purely a deliverance case, one of the clearest examples that we've seen of this need for the one ministering to be sensitive to the real needs of the individual, is that of a woman who came to us with terminal cancer. As soon as she was comfortably seated in the prayer room, I asked her simply, "What is it that you desire of the Lord?"

The woman began to sob, and then said, smiling through her tears, "You're the first one who has asked! I've been everywhere," she explained, mentioning several of the big names in healing. "And," she repeated herself, "You are the first one to ask me what I need! They all assumed that I wanted to be healed of the cancer and I do, of course. But," she continued earnestly, "what I really need is to know that I'll be with Jesus when I do die, whether it's cancer or something else that kills me."

How beautiful on her part, and how terribly sad on the part of those ministers who had allowed themselves to fall

---

[3]If you don't have the assurance of your own Salvation, I encourage you to order the cassette tape which is offered in the back of this book, "How to Be Saved, or Born Again!" If you cannot afford it, we will send it without charge.

into such an unthinking, uncompassionate pattern of routine that they failed to offer what should have been their number one message, the glorious Gospel of Salvation![4]

The Lord was about to expand our equipping by presenting a sobering truth....

---

[4]I don't wish to in any way minimize the importance of the truths in Scripture which A.B. Simpson so aptly described as the "Gospel of Healing." As one alive today only because of meeting Jesus as Healer, I firmly believe in healing. (The account of this miraculous healing is recounted in *Alive Again!*) It is definitely an important message which Jesus has entrusted to us. But it only has a *temporary bearing* upon one's life, while the Salvation issue is greater and is of *eternal significance*.

PART TWO

Demons Are No Joking Matter

Demons Are No Joking Matter

Case 4　　　　A Cocky Preacher Silenced

"I wasn't able to speak at all for three days, and even now I can't pray, can't read the Bible, and I can't say the name of Jesus!" Fear and torment were evident in the eyes of the normally very cocksure and brash young minister as he now spoke very humbly.

"How did this start?" He was asked.

"I asked some people to pray deliverance over me, one night in my home, just in case I needed it. As they were starting I noticed the clock on the wall and laughingly said, 'It's 12:00 — the witching hour.' I was struck dumb!" He sobbed, "And I feel completely cut off from God."

He was led in a prayer renouncing any opening given to the enemy through his joking statement, and then both the dumb spirit, and the spirit causing him to be unable to pray — that which had caused the wedge or blockage which he felt between him and God were cast out. He sobbed and sobbed profusely and then it was gone.

We can observe from this account that demons and deliverance are not something to be taken lightly nor to be played with. Satan and his minions take this warfare very seriously even if unsuspecting Christians and the world at large do not. The cocky minister's false bravado and joking reference to witchcraft might not have been so dangerous in a different setting...but when one is engaging the enemy in a battle for deliverance, Satan enters the arena prepared for battle: he is deadly serious. Unfortunately somewhat like a matador in the bullring turning his back upon the bull to show his disdain for his opponent, the young minister through his light-

hearted approach to the serious business at hand, had somehow lowered his defenses.

*** REVELATION: ***
DELIVERANCE IS NOT A GAME: NOR SOME-
THING TO BE PLAYED WITH JUST FOR EGO'S
SAKE.

OBSERVATIONS:

This account was unusual in that it was one of only a
very few cases that we've encountered in nearly 17 years
of involvement with the ministry of deliverance, wherein
the person apparently invited the spirit by mocking the
enemy. Yet it illustrates a basic, important truth — the
enemy is not to be taken lightly, nor underestimated. It
wasn't the only case we would encounter.

Insights / Giving Understanding:
WHY HAVEN'T ALL RECEIVED?

Honesty requires that we acknowledge that not all individuals seeking deliverance have received. The Lord has
granted understanding as to why in most cases. The reasons are often obvious: some who have sought help have
not really been serious: some have been so mentally ill or
disturbed when they came that they couldn't comprehend
what we were saying to them and were unable to make decisions to, for example, forgive. Many have come desiring
to have a 'magic wand' waved over them to make their problems disappear without any repentance, change, or effort
upon their own part, and still others have come under the
influence of drugs (usually prescribed by a psychiatrist),
again unable to comprehend or obey instructions.

Let me point out, that I can't recall a single case of a candidate who sincerely wanted deliverance, who was willing
to go through the steps, who humbled himself, and who
honestly faced his problems, that did not receive what he

desired. *God never has, nor will He, ever abandon an obedient child, nor one sincerely seeking Him.*

The truth I would have seen is that just because one hears of someone not getting delivered, doesn't mean that God has lost either His power or His desire to set His people free. What's been heard indicates somehow a failure on the human side of the issue. One thing I have learned, is that when I am not experiencing something that I see promised in Scripture as being available for believers, that the problem lies with me — there is something that I have failed to learn, something I haven't yet been taught, or some area where I am not in obedience to the Lord. The problem somehow lies on this side — for there has not been a power failure in Heaven!

You and I cannot see hearts and we don't know what really has gone on in the candidate, or if he even really wanted to be free. Once a woman brought her fiance' who supposedly had expressed a 'sincere' desire for Salvation and deliverance. When they arrived I soon grasped that he was high. I confronted him and asked if he had really quit taking drugs. He responded, "Sure, about two weeks ago."

I said, "I think you're high right now. When did you last do drugs?"

He admitted, "About two this morning. But I think I'm ready to quit, that's why I'm here. Besides, I think getting saved will help our relationship. We've been having some problems lately"

I then confronted the girl who brought him. She was a divorcee who had herself received a mighty deliverance from *suicide* and other powerful spirits and been Baptised in the Spirit years before. "Judy, you know better than this, John is really not ready for deliverance." She nodded silently in agreement.

I felt the old anger at Satan's work arising. "He mentioned 'your relationship,' is it righteous?"

"I don't know what you mean," she evaded.

"Yes you do. I can't talk to John about this because he

isn't expected to operate according to the same standards that you and I as believers are.''

''You are right, I do know what you mean, and the relationship isn't righteous. We've been sleeping together for six months. I know it's wrong and I know that it's sin.'' She admitted and blushed slightly.

''Well, you also know that God isn't about to have me pray deliverance just so your illict sex life can improve. You already know what you need to do about your relationship, don't you?'' She again nodded in agreement and repentance.

Turning to John, I explained, ''John, I don't think you can fully appreciate what I have to tell you about Jesus so long as you are high. If you are serious and if you decide that you do sincerely want to hear about Salvation, I will see you again at any time. But a relationship with God is too important to try to grasp under the influence of drugs.''

John has never called.

Deliverance is not to be taken lightly, neither is the freedom which is granted through deliverance. One must not only learn to walk in freedom, but to maintain it. (For suggested methods, see Personal Ministry Teaching Section ''Keeping Your Deliverance'' in Part Six.

We had already seen the danger of taking deliverance lightly, but we would see further dramatic proof as a result of events in a Missouri State Park....

Case 5   Violence in a State Park

Another case where problems arose as a result of thinking the subject of deliverance was a joking matter, involved a group of teenagers. Once again, the problems were incurred as a consequence of people playing with deliverance as if it were a game. This case is quite similar to that of the seven sons of Sceva who attempted to cast out demons in the name of Jesus, without having a right to the use of that name:

"Then certain of the vagabond Jews, exorcists, took upon them to call over them which had evil spirits the name of the Lord Jesus, saying We adjure you by Jesus whom Paul preacheth.

"And there were seven sons of one Sceva, a Jew, and chief of the priests, which did so.

"And the evil spirit answered and said, Jesus I know, and Paul I know; but who are ye?

"And the man in whom the evil spirit was leaped on them, and overcame them, and prevailed against them, so that they fled out of that house naked and wounded."

(Acts 19:13-16)

A group of about 30 young people in their late teens from a rural community about 80 miles south of our city had gone to a nearby State Park one Halloween evening after a party and decided to 'try deliverance' as they had seen it done in a movie.

They all stood in a circle on top of a hill in the state park and someone suggested that they cast demons out of one another. No sooner did the game begin than it ended abruptly — for they were all knocked from their feet and sent tumbling head over heels down the hill. None were seriously hurt, only scrapes and bruises occurred in the natural... but most of them picked up *spirits of terror, fear of demons and the Devil, torment* or at the least, other *spirits of fear*. A ministry in their town dealt with 28 of the 30 individuals, but then were unable to help the remaining two serious cases and called us for help. This occurred back in the early seventies, about 1973. We had scheduled a second deliverance conference to follow up on the one we'd had with Derek Prince the year earlier to introduce the validity of deliverance ministry to the St. Louis area. Don Basham was scheduled to be the main speaker but he called the day before the conference was to begin to tell us that his mother had just died and he would be unable to come. Since it was too late to call it off, we decided to go ahead with the deliverance conference and to use local men who were experienced in this type of ministry. So when the minister called, I said, "Sure, bring them down Sunday afternoon before the conference begins and we'll get ministry for them.''

At that time, I'd done very little deliverance ministry in public, only when thrust into it; when someone we were praying for for healing had gone into deliverance. The majority of our deliverance experience was in settings with no more than four people present. In light of this I had asked a man who'd ministered in deliverance longer than I, and was to be one of our speakers, to join us for the deliverance session. When were were ready to minister to the first young man, I turned to him and said, ''Brother _____ , why don't you take over and lead us,'' expecting to get a lesson from an ''old pro.''

Without moving from his chair he looked at me and said, ''No, Brother Bill, I feel you should handle this.''

I was surprised (shocked is more like it) by his suggestion, but I was by this point already accustomed to having the Lord thrust me into situations that I didn't feel I was ready for. I knew that the Lord was The Deliverer, that He wanted the young man free more than any of us did, and I was already feeling that inward anger against the enemy for what he'd done to these kids, and for flaunting his power over a powerless church!

So I led a prayer and then took authority over the spirits in the boy. Since the boy indicated that he hadn't a clue as to what his problem was, I commanded the first spirit to name itself. With absolutely no change of expression and no emotion, the boy responded out loud, *''Incest.''*

I was surprised at how quickly it had responded and slightly embarrassed, regretting that we had women present, but commanded it to leave anyway. There was absolutely no response. A moment later the Lord gave me a thought...perhaps cluing me in to the fact that he had displayed no remorse or embarrassment when he named the spirit, and so I asked him, ''Do you know what *incest* is?''

He replied, ''No, I've never heard that word before.''

In deference to the women present I walked over to him

and whispered in his ear, "Incest is having sexual relations with a member of your own family."

No more did I get the words out than it all broke loose. He let out a loud, growling groan and slipped out of the chair and onto the floor. A prolonged and dramatic battle ensued for two and a half hours. He went through physical gyrations that were impossible in the natural: he went up into a rigid 45 degree angle shape with his forehead on the floor and his toes on the floor, his posterior pointing at the ceiling and he bounced in that position. A little later he rolled over and curled up into a "U" shape with his navel on the floor and bounced up and down in that position for perhaps 15 minutes.

He writhed and rolled on the floor for about an hour longer before he was finally delivered. He sat up at last, wringing with sweat, and the church parlor smelling like a gym, but Praise be to God, he was free. You could tell it merely by looking at the joy beaming from his face, which moments before had been distorted into an almost bestial grimace.

The other boy was delivered in fairly short order after his root problem was uncovered and identified as also involving sexual perversion. He'd had sexual contact with an animal (bestiality) and later an homosexual encounter.

*** REVELATION: ***
INCEST WAS A SPIRIT IN THIS CASE.

*** REVELATION: ***
DEMONS CAN NAME THEMSELVES FROM WITHIN AN INDIVIDUAL, WHEN THE INDIVIDUAL ISN'T EVEN AWARE OF THE MEANING OF THEIR NAMES.

> ### *** REVELATION: ***
> DEMONS CAN IMPART VIOLENT, SUPERNAT-
> URAL MANIFESTATIONS.

OBSERVATION:

(A.)   Clearly there was a supernatural element involved here, in that the boy had never heard the term for the sin he'd committed, which was also the name by which the spirit identified itself out of his own mouth.

(B.)   The newly acquired spirits were apparently enabled to remain, because they were able to link-up with the stronger spirits already in place.

(C.)   The demon was able to cause manifestations which we would not have believed had we not seen them. This gives an indication of the great power which they can obtain within an individual who yields to them and cooperates with them because of the fear of having his sin exposed.

(D.)   Also to be clearly seen in this case is a demonstration of *the authority* given to us to cause demons to name themselves.

Insights / Giving Understanding: WHY SO LONG?

Why did it take two and a half hours to set this boy free? Why do some deliverances take so long? Why in the early days of our ministry in the area of deliverance did some take so very long, and were so violent and why today are they normally quicker and less violent?

I think that the Lord has revealed to us some of the answers.

In the preceding case, the boy did not come properly prepared for deliverance. As we will later see in the Personal Ministry Teaching Section, there are several steps one should take in preparing for deliverance; he'd missed several.

(1.)   He hadn't determined to be free of this spirit, and

had probably not even intended to mention it. Not recognizing that it was the source of his problem (or rather a root to which the new demons of *fear* and *torment* were able to firmly attach themselves), he was just hoping to lose what was tormenting him without expecting to confess fully his sins, or to be completely honest with either us or himself.

(2.)   Thus we were not only battling the spirits but also battling his will, which had not been set to break with this particular deeply entrenched spirit.

(3.)   We weren't as fully aware then as we are now of how great our authority and power in Jesus' name really is.

(4.)   We didn't realize then what we have since learned: that we can, for example, bind the *spirit of violence.* As a matter of battle tactics, it is wise to cast it out early in the deliverance. I learned this truth in a hurry when one woman picked up a chair intending to throw it at me.

The Lord was shortly to reveal more truth to us through a "related" case....

Case 6   Deliverance From a Homosexual Spirit

The same minister who brought the boy with incest phoned about three weeks later. I suspect faith had been built by seeing what the Lord had done in the previous deliverances. He wanted to know if he could schedule an appointment for a nephew from Arizona. He said "I've got a young man who is my twenty year old nephew. He's a fine young man who wants to come to you for deliverance from *homosexuality* if you're willing to try ministering to him. He's going to drive 1000 miles if you'll see him."

I again felt inadequate, but relying totally upon the power of *The Deliverer,* I said, "Okay," and we set up the appointment.

At the prearranged time, he arrived. I invited him into the prayer room and I was amazed. He was, without a doubt, one of the most handsome men I have ever seen. He had dark blonde hair, blue eyes, a nice complexion and perfect features. To look at him one would suspect that he was a model for men's shirts. He was strikingly good looking and there was absolutely nothing in his appearance, mannerism, nor his speech to indicate the problem that he had.

"I am a homosexual and I hate it!" he said emphatically. "I don't want to be one. Can you help?" he asked plaintively. "I have driven over a thousand miles to get here and I would have driven ten times that far if it meant I could be free. I have also been fasting for a week."

I must confess that my faith soared when I heard that. Hearing the difficulty that he had overcome, which was a strong indication both of the desperation and the depth of desire on his part to be free, I knew that God would not deny so sincere a seeker!

And his desire was not to be disappointed, for God did set him free. However, he did seem slightly disappointed when we finished. After he had forgiven those who had introduced him to homosexuality, confessed and renounced the sins involved and the *spirit of homosexuality* and the related spirits of *pornography* and *perversion* were cast out, he admitted, "I guess I am a little let down. I expected to bounce on the floor and that didn't happen to me."

What was the reason for the apparent ease of his deliverance? I believe, it was because *he was prepared for the deliverance*...and it had begun enroute...before he ever arrived at our prayer room. Perhaps it began when he decided to call his uncle, perhaps when he decided to fast, or maybe even before that, when he decided that he wanted to be free.

*** REVELATION: ***
DELIVERANCE BEGINS AS AN INTENT OF THE HEART.

> ### *** REVELATION: ***
> HOMOSEXUALITY WAS A DEMON AND WAS CAST OUT.

OBSERVATIONS:

(1.)   Just as sin (or yielding to Satan) begins as an intent of the heart, so too, freedom (or breaking with Satan) begins as a decision of the heart.

(2.)   Homosexuality was demonic in this case as most Christians might suspect, and most involved in deliverance already know.

A friend, who was an Assembly of God pastor, years ago shared with me an account of his having been led to minister to a teenage boy during a service. The boy had a long history of transvestite activity; would run away from home and later be found wearing lipstick, make-up and women's clothing. The boy was extremely effeminate and although almost twenty had never grown any facial hair nor needed to shave. My friend cast out the transvestite spirit and the boy was not only set free, but the next day had whiskers for the first time in his life. This gives an illustration of the physical effect which a demon can have upon an individual.

(3.)   Even though I felt inadequate, the demons had to respond to the authority and power of the Name of Jesus. Satan recognizes both his own limitations and the power in those opposing him....

TEACHING SECTION II

I. Satan Recognizes God's Workers

I. SATAN RECOGNIZES GOD'S WORKERS

Experience has functioned as a tremendous faith builder for deliverance. I firmly believe that the demons recognize what or how much we know. That is, they recognize our spiritual abilities, and our grasp of our authority. Just as they recognized the lack of the same in the seven sons of Sceva.

They would, I suspect, recognize me today as a more formidable opponent than they would have 17 years ago. This is not to exalt me, but simply to state that they apparently are aware of what we know about them. In much the same way that an experienced Marine would recognize the difference between the opposition being offered by green recruits and an army of seasoned, battle experienced soldiers, the demons recognize our capabilities.

The key missing for the Sons of Sceva, which we as Christians possess is *the right to the use of the name of Jesus;* ours through acceptance of Him and belief in His divinity and power. We enter the arena of spiritual warfare further equipped by the Holy Spirit who grants us discernment of spirits. The gift of discerning of spirits (I Cor. 12:10) is an enabling to perceive or distinguish (visually, mentally, or spiritually) the nature of the spirit being confronted. There are at least three categories of spirits which one might encounter. The reader should be praying for discernment even now as to whether what you are receiving is being presented under the anointing of the Holy Spirit, a human spirit, or that of an evil spirit.

Anytime someone professes to be speaking of the things of God, the true Christian should be praying for discernment. Paul encourages us in this regard, "But he that is spiritual judgeth all things." (I Cor 2:15) We must test and try the spirits, for any one of the three might be motivating the one speaking. If, indeed, it is the Holy Spirit your inner man should give you an inner witness, or confirmation of the validity of what is coming forth (your heart may thrill, you may get the Holy Ghost shivers, or you may just suddenly know!). If, instead, the human spirit were at work, the Spirit should warn you, revealing the flesh involved and allow you to realize that the one speaking is exalting himself, rather than Christ. Finally, if an evil spirit were motivating the speaker, and he began to teach, for example, on reincarnation, the Spirit would instantly give you a 'check in your spirit' concerning his doctrines.

Many Christians react with fear or abhorrence when the subject of Satan or demons is encountered. Although Satan loves that kind of reaction, Christians should be better informed. Satan is a defeated foe: Jesus has defeated Him upon Calvary's Cross, and has made provision for us to do the same. Each of us, however, following Jesus's example, must individually defeat him for ourselves. In addition Satan will ultimately be defeated by us, collectively, as the Church of Jesus Christ. "And the God of peace shall bruise Satan under your feet shortly." (Rom. 16:20)

Satan will be defeated under *our feet* by the only forces which he is bound to respect and before which he must ultimately bow: the anointing or empowering of the Holy Spirit and the Name of Jesus. The Name of Jesus utilized by those with a right to its use, is the only name Satan must acknowledge as the sons of Sceva learned to their chagrin.

Jesus desires that His followers be *Overcomers.* He has equipped us with the weapons for victory and even proclaimed it in advance in His Word:

> "And they overcame him by the blood of the Lamb,
> and by the word of their testimony; and they loved not
> their lives unto the death." (Rev. 12:11)

These victorious Christians defeated Satan by rejecting his blandishments, placing themselves under the Blood through Salvation, by witnessing and wooing others to Christ by their testimonies, and by even being willing to die if necessary for their commitment to Jesus.

The human will is sovereign, by God's design, and Satan cannot tread on a firmly fixed will. This explains why sometimes even a non-believing psychologist can get results: the candidate who makes a sincere decision to change and goes to the psychologist because he wants to break with his old life-style, puts muscle into that decision when he actually seeks help. Some people with potentially strong wills, who are capable of making such committed decisions, may find that source adequate. However the person whose will is not so strong, will probably only find his answer via the ministry of deliverance.

Jesus has granted power and authority to believers, but they must *will* to use that power to defeat him. The will of the candidate is likewise his key to victory in acquiring deliverance. God has not created us robots but rather as a people for Himself. We have the free will to succumb to sin and Satan or to resist and defeat him, thereby bringing honor and glory to our King.

There is no reason for Christians to fear either Satan or demons, even though we should recognize them as well prepared foes. The proper response on our part when we discover the reality of the existence of Satan's kingdom should not be that everything is demonic, any more than the equal error that nothing is demonic. Instead we should study the Word and prepare ourselves to properly engage in deliverance when needed.

* * * * * * *

The last case introduces another very important truth, that *it is not necessary for there to be outward, visible manifestations for a deliverance to be valid,* as Ed's account clearly showed us....

PART THREE

The "No Manifestation" Manifestation: Invisible Aspects of Deliverance

The "No Manifestation" Manifestation: Invisible Aspects of Deliverance

Case 7   Invisible Deliverance From Smoking

Another case illustrating the existence of the almost invisible aspect of deliverance is that of Ed. Ed, who had been saved, and received the Baptism in the Holy Spirit about a year prior, in the back room of our store, came for prayer for healing at one of our weekly public meetings. His eyes were bandaged, so that he was only able to look straight ahead. I asked Ed what he needed from the Lord, and he responded, "I need my eye muscles healed. I'm scheduled for an eye operation tomorrow morning."

His apprehension concerning his condition was evident in his expression. I invited Ed to be seated in the prayer chair, and as he moved past me, I smelled a terrifically strong aroma of stale cigar smoke. The scent was both strong and unnatural. I then asked Ed, whom I'd never seen smoke, "Do you smoke cigars? And if so, would you like to be delivered from smoking?"

Ed looked startled, but responded, "Yes I do, and I would definitely like to quit."

After we prayed for his healing, I then prayed against the *spirit of cigar smoking,* or *any other kind of smoking* commanding them to leave him. There was absolutely no reaction or manifestation of any spirit during or after the prayer, and I must confess that I had mixed feelings. I knew that I had tried to be obedient to the Spirit, and that the revelation of his smoking habit was supernatural. But thought perhaps I had misinterpreted the leading since nothing seemed to happen. We later heard that Ed had his operation the next morning, but we didn't hear from him.

53

A long time afterwards I received a phone call and recognized the cheerful voice of Ed. "Can you have lunch with me? I have some things I'd like to share with you." Unusually, my schedule was clear and so I agreed.

Over lunch Ed was bubbling with gratitude to the Lord, but he also profusely thanked me for taking the time about two years before to "answer the questions of an agnostic engineer," to explain Salvation to him, and for praying with him both for Salvation and the Baptism in the Spirit.

Ed then took a deep breath, and I could tell he was coming to the main purpose of our lunch. "Do you remember the night that I came for prayer for my eyes?"

I said, "Sure."

He continued, "That was nine months ago. Do you remember that you asked me a question?" (At the moment I didn't.) "You really shocked me when you asked me if I smoked cigars. I was dumbfounded, because I knew you couldn't have possibly known it, but I was then a chain smoker of cigars, pipes and cigarettes. I always had something burning."

He paused for a deep breath, and then went on. "The Lord showed me that I didn't have the faith to have my eyes healed. I know now that even if He had totally healed me that night, I would still have had the operation the next day, because my faith was in the doctors. But what I really wanted to tell you," now his eyes really sparkled, "is that the Lord completely delivered me that night from the *spirit of smoking!* I didn't realize it until two weeks after I got home from the hospital, when one night my wife said to me, 'Ed, how come you aren't smoking lately?' I then realized that I hadn't smoked, nor even wanted a cigarette, a cigar, nor a pipeful since the night you all prayed for me. He completely took the desire as well as the habit, and that has been nine months!"

Praise God for His faithfulness, even when we cannot see what is happening in either the spiritual or the physical realm. The proof of the deliverance was demonstrated in the freedom which he experienced in his life as he walked it out.

> ### *** REVELATION: ***
> GOD MAY GIVE SUPERNATURAL CLUES TO
> THE PRESENCE OF A SPIRIT.

> ### *** REVELATION: ***
> DELIVERANCE CAN OCCUR WITHOUT ANY
> OUTWARDLY OBSERVABLE SYMPTOMS OR
> MANIFESTATIONS.

OBSERVATIONS:

(1.) An important parenthetic revelation concerning healing is found here: God had shown him that he didn't have faith to be healed *because his faith was in a source other than God!*

(2.) The truth that God can give supernatural clues as to the presence of spirits has been confirmed to us in a variety of ways over the years, sometimes reflecting the Lord's sense of humor. One interesting and revealing case concerned a man in his sixties who, one evening in a private home, asked for prayer for help in finding his ministry. He admitted that he was mad at God for not giving him a full time ministry, after he had taken early retirement to make himself available to the Lord.

As we laid hands on him to pray for God's guidance for him, both my wife and I suddenly got a strong whiff of perspiration (it wasn't B.O. and lasted only a moment). I immediately cast out the spirit of works, and especially *sweaty works involving the flesh.* Ours, is to be a 'no sweat' religion: God instructed the priests in the Old Testament, that they were not to wear wool or anything that produced sweat. Jesus desires to be our burden bearer and instructs us to cease from our labors and enter into His rest: truly a no-sweat religion. Relying upon the Holy Spirit to do the supernatural work, takes all the straining out of our efforts.

Another beautiful example of the gentle, loving deliverance which God offers was given when God set Robert free from marijuana....

Case 8 Deliverance From the *Spirit of Marijuana*

Robert, a 17 year old, was brought to us for deliverance by his mother, who had caught him stealing drugs from his physician father's office. The mother had been begging, and cajoling her son for nearly a year to stop taking drugs. Since she had learned, on an earlier occasion, that he was stealing drugs from her husband's office drug cabinet, and then selling them to his school classmates to support his own marijuana habit. She became desperate enough to tell him (and to mean it) that she would turn him over to the police if it happened again. Upon catching him the second time, she offered him the alternative of coming for prayer or going directly to the police station. He chose us as the lesser of two evils. Needless to say, he was a less than eager candidate for deliverance, but nonetheless he came.

When he arrived, I asked if he wanted to be free of his marijuana habit. *Jesus has promised to deliver us from our enemies, but He has not promised to deliver us from our friends.* For this reason, it's very important, even essential, that the candidate for deliverance, desire to be free. Although it is probably possible to have someone delivered against their will, it would probably not be advisable since Jesus Himself warned of the latter state of such a person who returned to wallow in his sin, or who didn't seek to fill the house with more of God. Under other circumstances I probably wouldn't have attempted the deliverance, but the Lord was clearly in it.

He replied, ''No, I don't want to go to jail, but the marijuana doesn't affect me. I enjoy it, it doesn't hurt me, and I'll continue to use it.''

The problem most often connected with users of marijuana is the fact that they really don't believe that it has any negative effect upon them, and believe that it is harmless.

Unfortunately, various government agencies, and many private institutions, and even physicians over the years have told the public that marijuana is harmless. Giving a false sense of security about a substance that can do serious damage to the brain.

I knew if I was to be of any help to Robert I would have to help him see his need. So I removed the 'kid gloves': I bluntly asked him if he was aware that he was mentally impaired. "Are you aware that you are slow? The marijuana has affected your mental capacity and *you are slow!*"

His face flushed with anger, "I am not!" He retorted, "I am just as sharp today as ever!"

"What are your grades this year?" I asked, already aware from his mother that he had flunked out of school.

His voice dropped to a mere whisper as he responded, "D's and F's."

"What were they a year ago?" I continued the attack.

"A's and B's, but I'm still fine, I am not slow," he maintained.

I looked him straight in the eye and said bluntly, "Robert, I have never met you before, but I can tell that you've done drugs by the way it has affected your mind. I didn't know you before, so I could be judging you unjustly. For that reason, I want you now to look your mother in the eye and ask her if she doesn't think you are slower today that you were a year or so ago."

He turned somewhat self-righteously and said, "Mom, tell him that I'm not slow in ..." He stopped mid-sentence as he saw her tears.

She was indeed crying as she said, "I'm sorry Robert, but he's right. You are slow. Your grades used to be great, but now you're a terrible student and have flunked out of school." Praise God for her courage, and for the Lord's leading and moving in our conversation.

Robert turned back to face me humbly for the first time, and with true repentance said, "I'm sorry, you're right, it has affected me. I do want you to pray for me to be free from it."

Hallelujah! He was now in the right frame of mind and state of spirit to truly be a candidate for deliverance. We then prayed for his deliverance and commanded the *spirit of marijuana* to manifest itself and to leave him. As I addressed the *spirit of marijuana,* Robert opened his eyes and stared unseeingly at a point on the wall about two feet above my head. I touched his mother's arm and directed her attention to the one solitary tear moving slowly down his left cheek. When we were through, he accepted the Lord, received the Baptism in the Holy Spirit, and said that he felt terrific, as if a great weight had been lifted from his mind. I am firmly convinced that the true proof of the validity of deliverance ministry is fruit in the life affected. Robert had a job within two days, subsequently completed high school and college and is today doing very well, leading a productive life, continuing in a walk with the Lord.

*** REVELATION: ***
A SPECIFIC DRUG ADDICTING SPIRIT WAS CAST OUT, BY NAME.

*** REVELATION: ***
A SINGLE TEAR WAS THE ONLY MANIFESTATION OF A COMPLETED DELIVERANCE.

Insights / Giving Understanding:
WHY MANIFESTATIONS?

Another reason why greater manifestations were evident or manifested in our earlier experience with deliverance was, I believe, because God knew that we (those ministering) needed them, to fully convince us of how great the power at our disposal really was. I have seen in recent years — greater manifestations in our public meetings where apparently the Lord desires:

(a.) to demonstrate how great His power is through deliverance, and

(b.) to offer dramatic confirmation of His word, "with signs and wonders following," impressing the onlookers, just as occurred at Nain (Lk.7:15-16) and at Samaria (Acts 8:5-8).

Another possible reason for the more violent forms of deliverance is indicated in those cases where there hasn't been sufficient, or any, preparation on the part of the deliveree. I'm differentiating now between the true candidate for deliverance who is actively seeking deliverance, and comes expecting to receive it from the Lord, and the one who comes into a meeting unaware that deliverance will occur, and who is caught unprepared and off guard by the deliverance. In many instances the later category of individual may not even suspect beforehand that something like deliverance exists.

There are those who are sovereignly and suddenly thrust into an unplanned deliverance situation. This type is sovereign indeed. God...Who knows their need (while they may not), Who knows the solution (deliverance of which they may be totally unaware), and Who may have been subtly at work on them for quite a while preparing them — by showing them truths about themselves, about the source of their problems, revealing old hurts, about the need to forgive others, ...suddenly intervenes and sets them free.

In such cases we may not merely be battling the demon but also *the will of the individual* which in many cases is unaware of the existence of the demon. Therefore the unsuspecting candidate assumes that what the demon is doing, is actually a manifestation of his own personality, and he endeavors to protect or preserve that activity.

In Robert's case we cast out a single drug spirit by name, marijuana. However the Lord has shown us that there are different kinds of drug spirits and different ways of dealing with them....

59

TEACHING SECTION III
A Revelation Concerning Drug Spirits

I. Categorization of Drug Spirits
   A. Addiction
   B. Reaction
   C. Dependence

I. CATEGORIZATION OF DRUG SPIRITS

Drug spirits (or spirits associated with drugs) may be logically broken down into at least two basic categories: legal drugs and illegal drugs. One may become just as addicted to a legal drug as to an illegal drug. Let's consider the latter in more detail. The very fact that a drug is considered to be *illegal* tends to cause it's use to be associated with either *rebellion* or *disobedience*. The rebellion and disobedience may be directed at parents, society in general, or even at God. These facets of the problem will also need to be dealt with in those cases where their presence is indicated, or if they should manifest themselves.

We find that drug spirits may be cast out individually, by specific name when names are determinable, such as *marijuana* in Robert's case. Sometimes victims of drugs may honestly not know what the drug was, as in the case of something slipped into the punch at a party, or administered while already under the influence of drugs or alcohol. When the name of the drug is not specifically known, it can still be cast out, simply identifying it by either its manifestation or by its description such as the "blue and white pills that made me hallucinate."

There are, of course, also addictive spirits, and one may also specifically cast out addiction to a drug by name such the *spirit of addiction to heroin, marijuana, hashish, MJ, pot, cocaine, reds, blues, uppers, or downers*. It is usually advisable to use the same name by which the candidate has identified the drug, since that is the "handle" he has for it. If he's addicted to his "sleeping medication," then we don't need to call it by its true chemical name. Addictive spirits aren't limited merely to drugs or alcohol, but can also include addiction to sweets, such as chocolate or other types of food.[1]

---

[1]More truth concerning addictions to food substances, and how to deal with them will be found in the next book in this series, *Power for Deliverance: DELIVERANCE FROM FAT.*

An important revelation that the Lord gave us several years ago is that there are three entirely different types of problems related to drugs and demons associated with each category:

A. The obvious problem of addiction to a drug or drugs,

B. The problem of reaction to a drug or drugs.

C. The problem of dependence upon a drug or drugs.

A. ADDICTION

The first category of drug problem is fairly obvious, and most people involved with deliverance have, no doubt, been involved with praying for the deliverance of a candidate from one or more specific named drugs, such as marijuana or heroin. Since this is fairly self evident, we will not devote space here to this aspect.

B. REACTION

The second category came as a surprise to us. We first discovered it when we were asked to pray with a woman who was having all the skin rash symptoms which she had experienced while taking birth control medication about ten years before. She related that the Doctor had taken her off the medication due to her reaction, and she hadn't taken it since. However, she had sought prayer the previous evening for healing of her allergy to the drug, because she had been advised by a physician that he might again wish to have her take it.

We prayed for her healing, and as we did, we came against the *spirit of reaction to the drug by its name,* and commanded it to come out of her. (For example, if the name had been *aspirin* we'd have said, ''I command you *spirit of reaction to aspirin,* to come out of her.'') I was astounded a moment later when the young woman said, ''Look, I rubbed the areas on my arms while you were praying, and now look ... the rash and the scaling is all gone.''

To our amazement, when we looked, the areas she had shown us before praying that had been red and scaly were now identical with the rest of her flesh. Both deliverance and a miracle of healing in the disappearance of the symptoms had taken place when we had taken authority over the spirit causing the reaction. (Or perhaps the spirit when cast out had simply taken its symptoms with it.) The spirit had apparently been stirred up the previous evening when she'd received prayer for her allergy.

C. DEPENDENCE

The third category of drug problem also surprised us, but not as much, since we'd already seen the second category. This turned out to be *dependence upon a drug*. The incident which pinpointed it involved a friend who had sought prayer a few years before for a heart condition, and been totally healed. When he came this time for ministry, he said, "I know my heart trouble was healed several years ago when I was prayed for, however, I still have this problem: if I don't take my heart medication every day, I will fall asleep by 3 or 4 o'clock in the afternoon. I feel the problem is a spirit, since I've prayed about this for more than a year without relief."

We commanded the *spirit of dependence upon the drug, by its name*, to come out of him and to leave him forever. His testimony today, more than ten years later, is that he has had no recurrence of the sleepiness, even though the medication was terminated prior to the time we prayed.

*** REVELATION: ***
THERE ARE SPECIFIC DRUG SPIRITS WHOSE NAMES ARE THE SAME AS THE DRUG, AND THERE ARE ALSO SPIRITS OF ADDICTION TO THE SPECIFIC DRUG.

*** REVELATION: ***
THERE ARE SPIRITS OF REACTION TO SPECIF-
IC DRUGS.

*** REVELATION: ***
THERE ARE ALSO SPIRITS OF DEPENDENCE
UPON SPECIFIC DRUGS.

Exciting truths and yet we were about to learn of a force more powerful than drugs in its effect upon man and his health....

PART FOUR

Forgiveness Unlocks Doors of Deliverance

Forgiveness Unlocks Doors of Deliverance

Case 9   Crippling Overcome By Forgiveness

Sharon entered the meeting room in the hospital aided by two friends; they were half-dragging, half supporting her, one holding her under either arm. As they brought her in, her ankles dragged on the floor and her head flopped from side to side, but they finally managed to get her into a chair. My brother, who at that time worked as a director for the hospital, whispered, ''Isn't that a tragic case. She must be an MS (multiple sclerosis) patient or a birth defect case.''

I mentally agreed. However, I was distracted from my analysis of her condition almost immediately. I realized that I was being introduced by a local judge who, himself, had been healed of emphysema when we'd prayed in a similar service the previous year.

He completed the introduction, and asked me to share my testimony. I related the story of my miraculous healing from terminal cancer, gave an altar call for Salvation and then invited those who were sick or in pain to move forward that we might pray for them. I told those coming forward that as our custom was, we would not pray on a first-come, first-served basis, but would rather trust the Holy Spirit to give us the proper sequence in which to pray for those in need.

We prayed for several people with back pain, injured vertebrae, dislocated discs and the like. I was reminded of the first time we had been invited to speak and conduct a healing service in this hospital. I thought of the young nun who after an automobile accident, had five vertebrae surgically fused and was unable to stoop or bend to pick up her prayer books unaided, who had been beautifully healed. She had told us before we prayed, "I haven't been able to genuflex for five years." We had watched her kneel afterwards and stoop freely, bending and picking things up from the floor without any pain or difficulty.

As the service progressed and after a number of back problems had been healed, I noticed that the two friends were attempting to pull Sharon, the young girl I'd observed earlier, to her feet. I motioned for them to stop and wait. Sensing that she wasn't yet ready, I said, "Let's let her see a few more people healed before you bring her up."

About twenty minutes later, I felt it was time that she should come for prayer. When she was seated in the "prayer chair," I asked what she wanted Jesus to do for her.[1]

She replied, "I want to be healed, and to be able to walk like I used to."

I attempted to conceal my surprise, for I would never have suspected that she had ever been able to walk. And so I asked, "What happened to you...what is it that you need to be healed of?"

She responded, "I was in an automobile accident about three years ago."

For some reason I was led to ask her, "Have you forgiven the people who caused that accident?"

Her immediate answer without hesitation was, "Hell, no!"

When I didn't respond but merely continued to smile at her, she continued, now tearfully, "Would you forgive someone who did something like this to you? And besides," she said as if it settled the matter, once and for all, "they haven't asked to be forgiven!"

When I finished explaining forgiveness to her, I asked,

[1]Note: It is a good practice to have the candidate for healing specifically ask Jesus to heal them. It causes them to make a decision as to what they really want, puts them in the position of asking for themselves, and minimizes the role of the one praying for them.

"Are you ready now to make the decision to forgive them?"

"Nope!" She said firmly. "Besides everybody has prayed for me," the young girl stated almost proudly. "Even big-names like ... and ...." (She mentioned several names well known in the ministry of healing.) "...and nothing has happened, so I don't expect much from you either." She said with finality, as if to prepare me for the inevitable failure that would occur when I would attempt to pray for her.

"How did the accident happen?" I inquired trying a new approach.

"I was riding in the back seat of a car with my date. Another fellow was driving, in the front seat with his date. They were all drunk but me...my date tried to rape me. I put up such a fight...created such a ruckus...that the driver turned around to see what was happening and he ran head-on into an oncoming car. Both cars were totaled. All the drunks walked away without a scratch, and I was torn to pieces. They've already done five operations on me, but this is the best they can do. I still...can't even walk!"

"Will you forgive them now?" I pressed again.

"I will, if you will *guarantee me* that I will walk out of here tonight. If not, I won't," she stated flatly.

My reply surprised me, both with its firmness and its wisdom. "No, I can't guarantee you that you will walk out of here tonight, *if you do forgive them; but I can pretty well assure you that if you don't, you won't!*"

She reaffirmed her decision by shaking her head with her lips pinched tightly shut. So I told her to think it over, until she *was ready* to forgive them. We continued with the meeting and ministered to about a dozen more individuals who were healed. Then since we were out of candidates for prayer, I turned back to my stubborn friend, and asked once again, "Now are you ready to forgive them?"

She finally succumbed, nodding her head in agreement and said softly, "I'll try."

I led her in an audible prayer, forgiving the one who attempted to rape her, the ones who were drunk and didn't help her, the driver, the doctors who had been unable to really help her, and even God — whom she had blamed for letting it all happen. Then I proceeded to hold her feet[2] and prayed for her healing, at the same time breaking the hold of *unforgiveness* and *bitterness* commanding those spirits to leave. When I finished I had her repeat, "Thank you, Lord Jesus, for healing me."

When she had done so, I took her by the arm and said, "Let's take a little walk." I walked her once around the circle within the chairs (a distance of about 15-20 feet). She then asked, her voice trembling with excitement, "Am I walking, or are you walking me?"

I responded truthfully, "I am just lightly holding your elbow to steady you. You can try it alone."

She did: one lap around the circle gaining confidence with every step in what God had done for her. She then started toward a narrow aisle between the rows of folding chairs.

I laughed and asked, "Are you going to try an obstacle course?"

She replied, "Nope. I'm going home! Get my purse, Juanita, I'm going home!"

She walked out of that hospital; a walking testimonial not only to the power of our God to heal, but also to the tremendous power of Forgiveness.

*** REVELATION: ***
UNFORGIVENESS AND BITTERNESS TOWARD THOSE WHO HAD CAUSED THE ACCIDENT HAD BEEN A BLOCK TO HER HEALING.

OBSERVATIONS:

Even the doctors had been unable with five operations to help one who had bitterness and unforgiveness fester-

[2]Those unfamiliar with this form of ministry might be interested in a description of it to be found in the book *Alive Again!*

ing within her.

Sharon's healing was a tremendous faith-builder for all those who saw her go walking out of that hospital.

As powerful and full of truth as Sharon's story was, God still had more to show us concerning the *power of forgiveness...*

Case 10   The Power of Forgiveness Defeats Ulcers

I went to visit a member of our fellowship who had been taken to the hospital with severe abdominal pain. When I arrived at her room she explained that her condition had been diagnosed as severe inflammation of the pancreas, and at first they thought she had been poisoned. She told me that the doctors were planning to operate and remove her pancreas. We prayed, and the Lord immediately took all her pain. She then suggested that I step over and meet her roommate who was in for a stomach operation in connection with a severe ulcer condition.

I introduced myself to the roommate, a woman of about 50, who informed me she was in the hospital for her third ulcer operation. "I'm a Christian and I believe in healing. We used to belong to _____ Church, which was one of the biggest Pentecostal churches in the St. Louis area," she said with a tinge of what sounded like pride.

"You used to?" I asked, picking up on something in the way she'd said it.

"Yes, we haven't attended church since the big scandal broke. You, of course, have heard of the _____ Church and of Brother _____ ?"

"No," I apologized, "I'm afraid that I've never heard of either one."

"Well," she continued somewhat reluctantly, as if the memory was still very painful. "Several years ago, Brother _____ took the church for over a million dollars and disappeared. They still haven't caught him. The church exists, but it's only a shell. Most of the people are gone,

71

only a few oldtimers are left. My husband is now a broken man. The IRS called us in and couldn't believe we'd given the church as much of a tithe as we had. The IRS man said we were either liars or crazy to have contributed so much. That really hurt my husband. Afterwards he had a breakdown, and he's been on disability ever since. My sons were really 'turned off' to Christianity. One is married now, and goes to a church occasionally. The other wouldn't go near a church.''

As she spoke, I could feel the hurt and bitterness within this sister. I asked if her ulcer troubles had started at about the time the minister had absconded with the funds.

She thought for a moment, and then as understanding came, she nodded as if slightly embarrassed.

I smiled and said, ''You've got to forgive him for letting you down, for failing you, for hurting your husband, for driving your sons away from the church, and for every other pain and heartache that he's caused you.''

''I would like to,'' she said sincerely, ''but *what he did to my husband...!*''

''We often hurt more for our loved ones than we do for ourselves, and we often find it harder, therefore, to forgive hurts to them, than to ourselves.'' I tried to explain to her. ''But all the same you must, because this resentment and bitterness is destroying you. As an example of how malignant unforgiveness can be: right now, you and I could sit here and begin to think about what an evil man Hitler was. We could get our stomach juices flowing, get our blood pressure up thinking about how evil he was. We wouldn't be hurting Hitler, he's far beyond our ability to help him or harm him, but we would be hurting ourselves. The truth about hatred is that it tends to eat the one who has it.''

I glanced over to the other bed, and I noticed that our freshly healed sister was praying silently in the Spirit with us. The roommate looked up pitifully and said, ''I know you're right. I've known it all along. I've tried to convince

myself that I'd forgiven him, but I really haven't, and I know
I have to. Please pray with me, and help me forgive him.''
I explained the truths about forgiveness to her (see The Forgiveness Teaching Section which follows), led her through
the confession and prayer, and had her cast out every root
of *resentment, unforgiveness* and *bitterness.*

I was delighted to learn from our sister a week later,
when she returned to our weekly fellowship meeting, that
she herself had been totally healed and released from the
hospital by the doctors without surgery. I was doubly
blessed to also learn from her that her roommate's surgery
was canceled, and that she had gone home healed the day
following our prayer together rejoicing.

*** REVELATION: ***
BITTERNESS AND UNFORGIVENESS WERE NOT
ONLY BLOCKING HEALING, BUT IN THIS CASE
HAD ALSO CAUSED THE AFFLICTION.

*** REVELATION: ***
WE ARE OFTEN MORE DEEPLY HURT BY
WRONGS DONE TO OUR LOVED ONES THAN
TO OURSELVES, AND NEED TO FORGIVE THEIR
HURTS, AS WELL AS OUR OWN.

OBSERVATIONS:

(1.)   Applying the truth which we learned in Sharon's
case, we were able to help set this sister free from the *spirit
of unforgiveness* which was causing her affliction.

(Note)   We need to walk in forgiveness daily, dying to
self daily. Most often, unlike the case of our sister with
ulcers, the one causing our need to forgive is still around
and therefore the necessity of forgiving reoccurs. Thus we
need to make the decision each time we feel that we have
been wronged, to forgive that person or those persons

involved: even if that means doing it 70 X 7 times as Jesus said. When I am re-wronged, I quickly pray a simple prayer such as this:

Lord Jesus, I confess my hurt, my attitude, and my anger to you now as sin. I'm sorry for it and I ask you to forgive me for my sin of unforgiveness and this very instant, by a decision of my will, I choose to forgive _____ for what has just been done; and I ask that you forgive him also. I refuse to give unforgiveness any place in me, in Jesus' Name, amen.

"And be ye kind one to another, tenderhearted, *forgiving one another,* even as God for Christ's sake hath forgiven you." (Ephesians 4:32)

The next account underscores the necessity of forgiveness in obtaining, and maintaining wholeness and health...

Case 11   A Frozen Shoulder Freed

I was invited to speak at a home in Glendale several years ago. After I'd given my testimony, we began praying for healing and letting God confirm His Word with signs and wonders following. Shortly after we began praying for the people present one young woman, Ruth, came forward for prayer. She related that she had had pain in her lower back for about five years since being rear-ended in an automobile accident.

I was led to ask Ruth if she had forgiven the people who had caused the accident which injured her back. She admitted that she hadn't, even though she was already at that time a Spirit-filled, or Spirit-Baptized Christian. We led her in a prayer forgiving the people who had caused the wreck, and then prayed for the healing of her back. The pain left her back immediately, and she was able to move without any pain at all. Ruth ecstatically exclaimed, "This is the first time in five years that I have been completely free of pain in my back."

Ruth stood and watched until we'd finished praying for the other people present, and then she came over to me and inquired, "Say, what do you think the Lord can do

74

about this?''

She nodded toward her left shoulder and while attempting to raise it, could manage to get her left arm only about ten inches from her side.

I asked, ''What's the problem, a frozen shoulder?''

She said, ''Yeah, I guess so.''

''What has caused that?'' I inquired.

She replied, ''Well, I guess it's from the accident too, I've just had it all along.''

I wondered aloud, ''Why didn't you have us pray for it before?''

''Well, I just didn't think about it,'' she said simply. ''I've lived with this so long I didn't even think about it as an affliction to be prayed for.''

''That's fine, we're going to pray for you again.''

Ruth asked, ''Do you want me to sit back down in the prayer chair?''

''No, that isn't necessary,'' I responded. ''We'll pray for you right here.'' I started to anoint her, but then realized and explained to her, ''Since we've already anointed you once, there's no need to anoint you again. That other anointing with oil is still valid.''

Standing and facing her, I merely placed my hands on her shoulders and said, ''We're just going to pray for you right here.''

I began praying for Ruth, and within less than a minute, she began jerking and twitching. She raised one eyebrow, opening her eye and exclaimed, ''Hey, I'm having a reaction to your prayer.''

''Ruth, I don't think it's you. I think that's something within you reacting to the prayer, and,'' I went on, ''We're simply going to treat that thing as if it's a demon.''

She said, ''Okay.''

I began by praying, ''In the name of Jesus Christ we command whatever this is that's manifesting within our sister and causing this jerking to name itself and to come out of her.''

A gruff voice that didn't sound like hers hissed, "Hate."

I said to her, "Alright, Ruth, now we know what it is that we are dealing with, you command the spirit of hate to leave you."

Ruth said, "Okay, in the name of Jesus Christ, get out of me, you *spirit of HATE.*"

The word HATE came out of her mouth so loudly that the windows seemed to rattle. And it was gone. She said, "Wow, I felt that thing go. Praise God!"

As Ruth raised her arms in praise to the Lord who had just delivered her, she glanced at her left shoulder. Her face registering utter amazement, with one of the most shocked looks I've ever seen, for she could see that the frozen shoulder had instantly been made as whole as the other one. She was instantly healed, when the demon left.

I'm sure that we could have prayed over that shoulder for months and months, and probably never gotten anywhere; until we got to the root problem, which was a demon of hate, apparently directed toward the people who had caused the accident. When the demon was cast out, the healing took place. She was free, and she was whole.

*** REVELATION: ***
A SHOULDER WAS FROZEN BY A DEMON OF HATE.

OBSERVATIONS:

"Greater is He that's within you than he that's within the world," John has told us. That was demonstrated in this case and we find also a further illustration of a truth we've noted before, that *each time a demon is cast out, in the name of Jesus, it is a demonstration of the superiority of the Kingdom of God over the kingdom of Satan.* Deliverance is a demonstration, a flaunting of the impotence of the kingdom of Satan when it comes into conflict with the power of the living God, and the name of Jesus.

Forgiveness as we have seen is essential for those who desire to follow Jesus. Jesus considered forgiveness so important that every time He gave instructions for prayer, or conditions for answered prayer, He mentioned forgiveness. If He considers forgiveness that important, then we should better understand it than we do....

TEACHING SECTION IV

I. We Need to Better Understand God's Threefold Forgiveness
   A. God's Forgiveness of Us
   B. Our Forgiveness of Others
      1. Three Steps to Forgiveness
      2. Jesus' Own Forgiveness Teaching
   C. Forgiving Ourselves

I. WE NEED TO BETTER UNDERSTAND GOD'S THREEFOLD FORGIVENESS

Paul has told us that we are not to be ignorant of the wiles or the devices of the enemy. Many of us have been unaware that we even had an enemy, much less aware of the ways in which he can and does attack us. One of those ways is through our allowing unforgiveness and bitterness to remain within us. Warfare, in the natural realm, doesn't usually terminate when the last enemy soldier is killed, but rather, the battle ends when a particular conflict ends. Conflict may cease when one of several things occur:

1. The enemy withdraws from the battlefield,
2. A truce is signed, or
3. The enemy gives up on one front.

Often, this latter condition merely indicates a shift to a different theater of war, as was the case in World War II. When VE day came, the war really wasn't over yet, the area of combat simply shifted. The war officially ended on VJ day, or the signing of the peace treaty. But even then, the same hatred remained in the hearts of many people for years afterwards.

In fact, within recent years, a Japanese soldier was discovered hiding in the mountains of a remote island, who had never been informed that the war was over. If you or I had been shot by that uninformed soldier, we would be just as dead as if a full scale war were in operation.

The parallel is quite obvious. Our sincere belief that there isn't any war is not a defense against an enemy who is at war. Inaccurate theology won't protect us from our enemy Satan. His snipers are aware of the conflict and state of war, even if we have been told that the war ended, that all the enemy's weapons were destroyed at Calvary, and that he no longer exists as an enemy. Our erroneous theology, in no way impairs either his activities or his effectiveness. On the contrary, it enhances it, as it allows him to operate in a virtual cloak of invisibility.

So long as we deny his existence, he can strike us practically at will. If we don't realize that we have an enemy, we are almost totally vulnerable to his attacks. What is even worse, when trouble comes we often assume that we have in some way displeased God, and that He is afflicting us for some 'higher purpose.' God, unfortunately, often seems to get a black eye in the minds of many people because they attribute to God the Father the works that have actually been done by Satan.

There is a specific wile of the enemy that is particularly nasty, because it works *inside us*, insidiously from within, like a Fifth Column force. It gets inside us, and we don't even want to admit that it is there, but it is. This enemy is UNFORGIVENESS.

GOD'S THREEFOLD FORGIVENESS

The solution to this problem is three-fold forgiveness: one, our own forgiveness at the hand of God; two, our forgiveness of others; and three, our forgiveness of ourselves.

A. God's Forgiveness of Us

"I, even I, am He that blotteth out thy transgressions for My own sake, and will not remember thy sins."
(Isa. 43:25)
"For I will forgive their iniquity, and I'll remember their sin no more." (Jer. 31:34)
"He will have compassion upon us and will cast all their sins into the depths of the sea." (Mic. 7:19)
"For thou hast cast all my sins behind thy back."
(Isa. 38:17)

God has made a series of mind-staggering promises concerning His forgiveness. In the Old Testament He made a fantastic promise: He said that as good as the forgiveness which He had offered previously had been, it was going to get even better. He said that when the Messiah (Jesus) came, if we would but confess our sins unto Him ... that then He (God the Father) would cast our sins behind His

80

back, and into the depths of the Sea of Forgetfulness. In other words, God said He would see our sins no more. As great as that is, it gets still better: He also tells us that *He will remember our sins no more.*

These are truly mind-boggling promises. Here we have the Word of God Himself, that if we would but confess our sins to Jesus, that then He, God the Father, *would neither see nor remember our sins any longer.* Our minds literally stagger at the implications of these promises: if my sins no longer exist in either the sight, or the mind of God ... then I would certainly be foolish to worry about them. In fact, if they don't exist in the sight or mind of God, they truly do not exist at all. I need never be concerned about them again. I have in truth, as Paul says in the New Testament, been "justified." I have become, *just-as-if-I'd* never committed the sin in the first place. Once I repent of it, and confess my sin to Jesus, it becomes just as if it had never happened!

Paul also says that the blood of Jesus Christ cleanses me from all unrighteousness. This means that if you were to take a blackboard, and list upon it all my sins, the blood of Jesus would still cleanse me from all unrighteousness. The effect is greater than if you were to take a wet towel and wash the slate clean. All my sins are eliminated, done away with completely by the Blood of the Cross. The slate is truly cleaned. It is just as if I'd never sinned in the first place. This, in simple terms, is what "justification" is all about. Hallelujah!

To apply this principle to our present consideration, once the sin of unforgiveness, bitterness, hatred or any other sin is repented of and confessed to Jesus as sin, then I am clean, and in God's sight, it becomes just as if it had never happened in the first place. By His own word He can no longer see nor remember that sin any longer. I am truly a New Creature, and it is a whole new ball game!

FORGIVENESS, NO MATTER HOW BIG
OR NUMEROUS MY SINS

In Matthew 18, we see a further expansion of the fantastic forgiveness of God. Jesus told Peter, when He was asked, "Must I forgive my brother seven times?" Not merely seven times, but rather "seventy times seven" times, or an infinite number of times. Jesus also said elsewhere, that the servant is not above his master, thus He tells us that we must forgive our brothers a limitless number of times, then He too must be *willing to forgive us a limitless number of times.* His forgiveness is truly infinite.

> "Though your sins be as scarlet, they shall be as white as snow," (Isa. 1:18)]

Nothing is too difficult for God. He can, and desires, to forgive all your sins if you will repent, and turn to him.

B. Our Forgiveness of Others

Forgiveness of others is necessary if we are to go on with God. It is essential that we forgive those who have hurt us or wronged us. Anyone who has hurt you badly enough, for example, to make you cry, might be a logical candidate for your list of those to forgive. Whether the person is now living or dead is irrelevant. We must forgive to remain righteous before God and rightly related to Him.

The Scriptural basis for this is found in Jesus' own words:

> "And when you stand praying forgive, if you have ought against any, that your Father also which is in heaven may forgive you your trespasses." (Mk. 11:25)

It is also found in the words of Paul,

> "Forebearing one another and forgiving one another. If any man have a quarrel against any, even as Christ forgave you, so also do ye." (Col. 3:13)
> "And be ye kind one to another, tenderhearted, forgiving one another, even as God for Christ's sake hath forgiven you." (Eph. 4:32).

1. Three Steps to Forgiveness

The Lord has shown us over the years, through many examples, that there are at least three natural steps to accomplish forgiveness. These three natural steps are our responsibility and precede the fourth step which is a supernatural activity, and is therefore God's responsibility. The fourth step is the miracle step which changes hearts, and makes situations change and become right. The three natural steps are prerequisites to true forgiveness.

Step 1. CONFESS THE UNFORGIVENESS, OR BITTERNESS, OR HATRED AS SIN. Because that is how God views it.

Step 2. RENOUNCE THE UNFORGIVENESS, OR BITTERNESS, OR HATRED. Make the decision to break fully with the unforgiveness. ("Can two walk together unless they be agreed." Amos 3:3) We must make the decision not to walk in agreement with Satan or any of his works, or any other work of darkness: to sever ourselves from any and all ties with him.

Step 3. MAKE THE DECISION WITH YOUR MIND, AND CONFESS IT WITH YOUR MOUTH, TO FORGIVE THAT PERSON, OR THOSE PERSONS WHO HAVE HURT YOU OR WRONGED YOU, (Forgive them each by name, individually and specifically,) AND ASK THE LORD TO FORGIVE THEM.

Having done these three natural steps, we can then rightfully expect the Lord to sovereignly do the fourth step, the miraculous part of this ministry, and take all the unforgiveness, all the bitterness, all the hatred, pain, resentment, hardness of heart, anger, hurt, rejection, and all the poison out of these relationships.

2. Jesus' Own Forgiveness Teaching

Jesus, Himself, gave the best teaching on forgiveness, and He gave it from the Cross. He gave it when He prayed, "Father forgive them for they know not what they do."

Consider for a moment what He was really doing. We say, "I'll forgive so and so if he changes." Or, "I'll forgive what's his name, if he asks my forgiveness, or if he apologizes." None of these conditions had been met by those whom Jesus chose to forgive that day. He forgave them: (1) While they were still in the process of doing the thing for which He was forgiving them; (2) They hadn't changed; (3) They hadn't asked His forgiveness; (4) They were still inflicting pain upon Him; (5) They were still hurting Him, literally to the point of death; and yet (6) He forgave them; and (7) He asked the Father to forgive them also.

We can note these seven unique facets of the forgiveness teaching which Jesus, in effect, was giving to us. The seventh point bears a special note. He not only forgave them, Himself, but He also prayed and asked the Father to forgive them!

We can't allow ourselves to be like the little old lady with whom I spent nearly an hour attempting to convince her of the need to forgive someone who had wronged her. (Bitterness was ruining her life; all her family could see it, but she wouldn't admit it.) When I asked her if she hated anyone, she replied "Of course, I don't hate anyone, Honey, I am a Christian!" (Christians, of course, never *hate* anyone.)

Finally I asked, "Whom do you like the least?"

Then the bitterness poured forth as if a dam had burst, "My brother!" The story of every wrong or slight which he had committed against her during the past twenty years came out in detail. Still when questioned she wouldn't admit any hatred. Only with much coaxing did she finally admit to "Perhaps, slight dislike."

So I suggested, "Well, why don't we forgive him anyway for all these wrongs that he's done to you over the years?"

She replied, "Oh yes, Honey, I do forgive him...because 'Vengeance is mine saith the Lord'... and He can get him far better than I ever could!"

Needless to say, she wasn't yet ready to really pray for his forgiveness.

C. Forgiving Ourselves

There is a third area of forgiveness. In addition to the forgiveness which we ourselves receive from God, and the forgiving which we must do of others, there is also the matter of forgiving ourselves. Once again, rather than giving you my opinion on the subject, let me share with you this truth just the way the Lord taught it to me.

This truth came the first time the Lord ever gave me a "prophecy." As is so often the case, if God does something in a way that is new or unfamiliar to us we immediately assume "That can't be God." That's what I assumed. I was preparing my notes one afternoon for a teaching I was to give that same evening on forgiveness, and I received a prophecy concerning forgiveness.

When the prophecy came into my mind, I immediately thought, "Wow, this must be God...because I know that I couldn't have come up with a beautiful thought like that: phrased like that, and besides it certainly sounds like something that God would say. So true, and so beautifully simple."

It was obvious to me that the message was clearly beyond my wisdom, but still it didn't come to me in the way that I had heard prophecy should come. I'd always heard that if someone were supposed to give a message in prophecy that they would either hear an audible voice, or they would shake all over, or their skin would tingle, or that something equally out of the ordinary would occur. Somehow the person would be informed that they were to speak out the word, and it would happen right on the spot, not hours beforehand.

Because none of these phenomena attended my series of thoughts I concluded that it must not be a "real" prophecy. Still, it was so good that I told the Lord prayerfully that since it didn't come to me in the manner I felt it should have, that I would put it in my notes anyway with a box around it, and when I got to the point in my teaching where I felt it should have fit in, I would wait for the "anointing" which I considered necessary to confirm the prophecy's validity for me, and I would give it to the group. If, however, the anointing did not come, then I would conclude that I had misinterpreted His intentions, and would pass over it.

That evening I finally reached the point in my notes where the box appeared, and I paused awaiting the anticipated anointing ... and nothing happened. No unusual feelings at all, so I passed over the "prophecy" and continued my teaching on the subject of forgiveness. When the meeting was over and most of the people had left the room, one young man came over to me and said in low tones, "I really appreciated the things you had to say tonight about God's forgiveness, I needed to hear them. But my problem isn't so much with God forgiving me, as it is with *me forgiving myself.* I did things while in college that I still haven't been able to tell my wife about to this day, and I cannot forgive myself!"

I interrupted him at that point and said, "Wait a minute, Brother, I have missed the Lord tonight, because I had a prophecy for you that I didn't give. It speaks exactly to what you've just said, let me get it and I'll read it to you." I then read him the prophecy which went something like this:

> "There are those here tonight who have asked Me to forgive their sins. Yet you are still going around bowed under the weight of your sins. — You have asked Me to forgive you of your sins: *I have* forgiven you. I *have* taken your sins from you. You can stop asking Me. They aren't your sins anymore: you have given them to Me: they are Mine! .... Now *you* get *your* hands off *My* sins!"

The young man's eyes filled with tears, and he said, "Wow! That word was directly for me. That describes my situation perfectly. Thank you."

The next week I belatedly shared the prophecy with the

entire group. Again, several people came up afterward with the same kind of reactions. They came with tears of joy, to thank me for sharing the words, as they had spoken directly to their hearts as well. There has been such an anointing upon this prophecy, or truth, that every time I've been led to relate this story as I've traveled and taught around the country, the reaction has been almost identical. People invariably come forward to tell me that they really needed to hear those words, and that God had touched their hearts, and brought relief and release with His message.

God so desires to minister to His people, and to bless them, that he will even use a "doubting-prophet."

* * * * * * *

Ruth's story in the previous case illustrates beautifully another truth: *that healing and deliverance can be integrally related and are often interdependent.* Both healing and deliverance are manifestations of the love and sovereignty of God. The following accounts may well provide a whole new appreciation for the sovereignty of God....

PART FIVE

The Sovereignty of God: Faith-Building Truths

The Sovereignty of God: Faith-Building Truths

There are truths that tend to build our faith in God to perform the supernatural in response to our prayers, or to seek Him boldly for supernatural solutions to our problems. My own faith has been given a tremendous boost by some of the cases we have already considered but the following illustrate powerfully the supernatural aspect of *God's Ministry, Timing,* and *Provision,* and especially His *Omnipotence, Omnipresence,* and *Omniscience.*

THE SUPERNATURAL ASPECT OF *GOD'S MINISTRY:*
Case 12   Joe in Trouble

Joe arrived at my office looking troubled and slightly scared but more desperate than anything else.

"Why have you come to see me, Joe?" I asked.

"I've got problems. Last night I beat up my fiance. I really love her, but I beat her up again last night." (I had seen the girl's 'shiner' earlier when they had come in together.) "I've always been able to handle things on my own, but I can't handle this...I shouldn't be hurting the people I love...I need help, and I guess, I must need Jesus!"

I was touched by Joe's humility and honesty and gladly explained Salvation to him. When I inquired if he would like an opportunity to accept Jesus and invite him into his heart, Joe's eyes filled with tears as he said, "Yes."

I led Joe in a responsive prayer of Salvation. When the prayer was concluded, I opened my eyes and looked at Joe. His head was still bowed, cradled in his arms on my desk and he was visibly trembling. I thought I recognized the symptoms, but he was really a literal babe in Christ. He's probably never heard of the Baptism in the Holy Spirit, I argued with myself. However, since his head remained bowed and he continued to tremble, I went ahead and asked, "Would you like to receive the Baptism in the Holy Spirit?"

Joe nodded in the affirmative, so I told him to just pray and ask Jesus to baptise him with the Holy Spirit. He did so. Next I instructed him to "just open his mouth and..." (before I could even suggest that he "tell Jesus that he loved him without saying it in English")...He began praying fluently in tongues.

I asked Joe afterwards, "Have you ever heard of the Baptism in the Holy Spirit before today?"

"No. I'd never heard of it until you just mentioned it a few moments ago," he said simply.

"Have you ever heard of 'speaking in tongues,' or read about it in the Bible? Or do you know what 'tongues' are?" I queried, my curiosity aroused.

"No. And I've never read the Bible, In fact, I've never been to a church either," he added.

"Do you know what you were just doing or saying? Had you ever heard any of those words before which you just spoke?"

"No, I don't. I couldn't understand a word that I was saying. What was that all about?" Joe inquired, turning the tables on me.

I was so blessed that I could hardly speak, realizing that I had just witnessed a sovereign 'house of Cornelius' type Baptism in the Holy Spirit (See Acts Chapters 10 & 11). No one had ever explained anything to Joe. No critic could challenge that he had been 'taught' to speak in tongues, or that he'd been 'psyched up' to expect it, or that he was a 'religious fanatic,' being a completely un-churched, un-Bibled, brand-new Christian babe.

We then prayed for Joe to be set completely free of his *anger, temper, spirit of violence, spirit of hatred* and *abuse of women,* and anything else *that would cause him to hurt the ones whom he loved.* He was set free. Today Joe has a family and is still married to the same woman who brought him in for ministry more than ten years ago.

*** REVELATION: ***
BAPTISM IN THE HOLY SPIRIT, CONFIRMED WITH TONGUES, SOVEREIGNLY BESTOWED BY GOD ON ONE WHO HAD NEVER EVEN HEARD OF IT.

THE *TIMING* AND *PROVISION* OF GOD:
Case 13   **Kathy in Prison**

Kathy's story blesses me everytime I recall how unbelieveably, perfectly God dove-tailed the details of His timing and provision to make possible the delivering of a woman from the *spirit of suicide,* the receiving the Baptism of the Holy Spirit by another woman behind bars, the opening of a prison to the ministry of the Spirit, the creation of a new ministry within the walls of a prison, the saving of her children in response to prayer, and the arranging of all the details to bring us together.

One Tuesday evening, a dozen years or more ago, a woman came to our store right at closing time, desperately seeking help. One of the girls came and got me out of the back and said that a woman needed prayer and that she was suicidal.

I went out and met the woman, who identified herself as Samantha Smith. "Samantha," I asked, "Why are you suicidal?"

She sobbed out her story, "Well, my sister-in-law has murdered my brother. My brother was the only living relative that I had. We were orphaned as children. He and I grew up together, and we were the sole support of one another. We comforted one another, and we were more than just brother and sister, we were mother and father for one another." She paused to wipe away tears with a tissue and then continued, "The closest person in this world to me was my brother, and she murdered him." Samantha gritted through clenched teeth.

As her story came out, and as she mentioned the names involved I remembered the case which had made headlines in the newspapers for several months. The Missouri newspapers had a field day with the bizarre case of the St. Louis County detective who had been "murdered by his wife." They reported that she had apparently killed him "by feeding him arsenic which had been added to either his soup or his wine." The case was rather confusing. There had been all kinds of charges, counter charges, and denials. But ultimately the sister-in-law of Samantha, was adjudged to be guilty, convicted and sent to prison.

As I talked with Samantha, I shared with her that the hatred she had was eating her, and would eventually destroy her.

"I know it." she said. "As a Christian, I know I shouldn't hate. I used to be a Christian, but since all this has come up, I'm not even sure I'm a Christian anymore," she sobbed. "I just hate her." The hatred was eating her alive.

To make a long story short, we shared with her the truth and teaching about forgiveness, presented in Teaching Section IV, and Samantha finally came to the point of making a decision to forgive her sister-in-law for murdering her brother, the person whom she loved more than anything else on this earth. The *spirits of hate, murderous hate, retaliatory hate,* and *suicide* were cast out.

Samantha then asked, "Now can I receive the Baptism in the Holy Spirit?"

"I think that's probably exactly what you need." I agreed. We prayed with Samantha and she received the Baptism in the Holy Spirit. She left the prayer room that evening rejoicing to be free of the weight of the sins of hate, unforgiveness, and bitterness that had been eating her, and also rejoicing in the fact that she had a new prayer language.

That was Tuesday night. The following Saturday evening I was scheduled to speak at the Ramada Inn in Sedalia, Mo., for the Full Gospel Business Men's Fellowship. However, when I awoke Saturday morning it was obvious to me that I was under a Satanic attack: I was so dizzy I could barely stand up. I had been fine the night before, but that morning I knew I couldn't make the three or four hours drive down to Sedalia. So I called Jim, a friend from our fellowship, and asked if he would be willing to go along and do the driving? He graciously said, "Sure."

By way of background our fellowship was praying at that time for the Lord to open a way for us to get Bibles and books into the Missouri Prison for Women located at Tipton, Missouri. We had been furnishing Bibles, Christian books and tapes to most of the other prisons in the State. At one point we'd even sent a minister around to visit the Chaplains at each prison, to arrange for us to be able to supply the prisoners with Christian materials. We had received a warm response from most of the other prisons in the State, but the one prison we had been unable to get a break through with was the Women's Prison at Tipton.

We had been seriously praying about that, because we felt, "There are all those women shut up behind bars, that need Bibles, and the ministry available through books like the rest of the prisoners," but we had been unable to get through to them. Since Tipton was located near Sedalia, I had hoped that perhaps the Lord would let me get by there personally. But as things looked that Saturday morning, I had little hope of making any side trips.

Late Saturday afternoon we arrived in Sedalia at the Ramada Inn. I walked up to the counter, and asked the young female clerk behind the counter for the room reserved for 'Banks.'

She checked and said, "I'm terribly sorry, but we don't have a room reserved for 'Banks.' "

"There has to be one: the Full Gospel Business Men may

have it in their name. They reserved the room for me here tonight. I'm to be the speaker at the Full Gospel meeting." I explained thinking that they might have a room reserved just for "speaker," as sometimes happens. She said, "Well I know about the meeting, but there is no room reserved for you."

I replied, "Well that's okay, just give me another room."

The girl snorted, "You've got to be kidding."

I asked, "What do you mean?"

She chuckled, "This is State Fair weekend, and there isn't a room within sixty miles of here."

I said, "Well, go check the cancellations."

"I just checked the cancellations when you asked me to look for your room." She said, "There aren't even any cancellations."

I thought to myself, 'Wait a minute, something is going on here.' And in a little burst of faith I said, "Please, go check again."

The girl went begrudgingly back into the back room, and returned with a look of disbelief upon her face, and said, "You're not going to believe this, but we just received a cancellation."

I said, "It's a double, isn't it?"

By now it was all really beyond her and she shouted, "How did you know?" I told Jim later that I knew it had to be a double, because the Lord wasn't going to make him sleep on the floor. He laughed, enjoying thoroughly the supernatural aspect of our trip.

After changing clothes, we went on to the meeting. Before dinner began, the president mentioned to me that the following morning, was to be their monthly Sunday service out at Tipton prison and he wanted to know if I would like to go along and minister to the prisoners.

I said, "That would be great, because our fellowship has been praying for a way to help the women in Tipton for more than a year. But I'll have to ask Jim, because he's my transportation."

Jim called his wife, to check. After clearing it with her, he returned and said, "Sure, it'll be fine."

The president then asked, "By the way, did you notice the two women sitting in the front row?" We observed two heavy-set women, a sweet-face black woman and an older white woman seated in the front row. He continued, "Those two are here tonight on special pass from Tipton Prison to attend this meeting."

We began sensing in our spirits that God was about to really do something. After I shared the testimony of my own healing, I began praying for healing for those present. Beautifully enough, the Lord arranged to have both of the prisoners get healed. The sweet faced black lady had a long standing back condition which the Lord healed. After the meeting was over, she came up to me, and asked, "Would there be any possible way you could come out to the prison, tomorrow, and minister to some of the women there? There's a lot of them that really need prayer."

I gladly responded, "We're planning to be out there tomorrow. They've asked me to come out and minister in the morning."

She said, "Well that's wonderful."

Early the next morning we drove out to the prison. By the time we arrived, the women were already seated in the room. Several other gentlemen and I sat in the back, while the president of the chapter went up front and started the meeting with a hymn. He then had an opening prayer, and introduced someone who was going to complete a 'brief teaching' that they'd begun the month before.

God bless him, the man was sincere, but his teaching, was so deep and dry that most of it was going over my head. As a base of reference, I have a college education, have taken Biblical courses at the college level, and still he was going over my head. So if it was difficult for me to follow what he was trying to teach, I knew it was being totally lost on these poor women, some of whom could probably barely read. But he went on, and he went on, and he went on.

The service was only to last 45 minutes. Forty minutes later he was still talking.

I had a quick conference with the Lord, I prayed, "Lord why are you allowing this guy to talk so long? Can't you get him off." That may not sound very spiritual or kind, but that's the way it was. In any event, I continued praying, "Lord, you didn't arrange all these miracles, like getting us the motel room and into this prison, to just listen to this guy talk about stuff that's going over their heads. You've got me here, I assume, to minister to someone, to pray for healing, or for Salvation, or the Baptism in the Spirit, to share my testimony or something fruitful. Instead, I'm sitting here in the back trying to stay awake listening to this man teach." He droned on and on. Finally a lady guard stuck her head in the door and said loudly, "You people have taken too long! You've got to leave right now, there's another group going to come in to use this room."

I thought, "Somehow I, or someone, must have really missed the Lord in this whole thing."

The president interrupted the speaker and said, "Well, we'll have to break." He offered a closing prayer, and the women all start filing out. All I could do was stand there and politely shake hands with them as they left. I was feeling, "this is all a bad dream, there's something wrong here."

At about that time, the guard stuck her head back in the room, and said critically, "Oh, you people have taken so long, the other group had to go to another room, if you want to stay a few more minutes, you can." Most of the women had already left. I was at a loss trying to comprehend what had taken place, when suddenly I felt a tap on my shoulder. I turned around to see my sweet-faced black friend from the night before who had a back healing. She said, "Hello, Brother Bill."

I replied, "Well, how are you? And how's the back?"

"Oh, my back is fine." she responded. "But I'd like you to meet Kathy. Kathy needs prayer."

I looked over her shoulder and saw Kathy who had her arm in an ace bandage. I thought to myself, "At last, here's a chance to finally pray for healing."

We found a quiet corner of the room, where I invited Kathy to sit down, and asked, "Okay, Kathy, would you like prayer for your arm?"

She said, "No, my arm is fine."

Taken aback, I asked, "Well what would you like prayer for?"

She said, "I'd like prayer for my children. Since I've been in here my children have been in foster care, and my sister-in-law is trying to take my kids away from me and adopt them, and I don't want that to happen. So I'd like you to pray that my kids not be adopted by my sister-in-law."

All of a sudden the nape hair on the back of my neck began to stand up, and I asked her, "Does the name Samantha Smith mean anything to you?"

She didn't react at all. As if expecting the Lord to have told me her sister-in-laws' name, she simply responded, "Yeah, that's my sister-in-law."

I thought, "Wow!" I got goose bumps on top of my goose bumps, when I realized what God had done. He'd arranged sovereignly for the sister-in-law of this woman to come, out of all the places she could have gone, to me and my prayer room for prayer, for her suicidal state, in order that she might forgive this woman in prison, and then God arranged to get me into the prison to tell her that she had been forgiven. Isn't that wild?

I shared all that with Kathy, who then asked for and received the Baptism in the Holy Spirit, after we prayed for her children's well-being. Since that time the Lord has mightily used her within the prison system in starting a ministry of prisoners to prisoners, and starting a Bible study for prisoners that spread throughout the prison system. Her activities were written up in a national prison magazine, and she has managed to touch hundreds, if not thousands, of lives since she herself was touched by the Lord.

We have shipped hundreds of Bibles into Tipton prison, and now since Tipton has been closed, we ship Bibles for her to prisoners in other prisons. One year we were able to ship Christmas presents to the children, of all the women in the prison. We sent a list to them, and let the women select what their children needed, Bible story books, Bibles or whatever. Let's briefly summarize what God did in this case — the mighty way God worked, arranged, and dovetailed all the details, in making possible our meeting, and Kathy being Baptized in the Holy Spirit:

* Samantha came the Tuesday *before* I went to Sedalia. She could have come the week after, she could have gone anywhere else, but she came *to our store the Tuesday before.*

* She came *to my prayer room* instead of somebody else's.

* She was willing *to forgive Kathy.*

* Jim just happened *to be available* to drive me down there.

* We just happened *to get the last room* in Sedalia, enabling us to stay over.

* The women from the prison just happened *to be there* the Full Gospel Meeting on pass, and just happened *to get healed.*

* I just happened *to be their speaker.*

* And it just happened to be the Full Gospel's time of the month *to have their meeting at the prison.*

* They just happened *to invite me to the prison.*

* Jim just happened *to be able to stay over.*

* The black woman just happened *to run into Kathy* outside the chapel and to bring her in.

* Kathy just happened *to ask for prayer.*

* The Lord just happened *to have me ask her name.*

As a result of all these coincidences that God so beautifully arranged, He raised up a ministry behind prison bars, and has changed many lives. Kathy's son is now a minister. It boggles the mind to see all the fruit God has brought forth out of the praying for Tipton Prison.

There is a final 'looney tune' to this whole fantastic story. God who so often and so beautifully arranges coincidences, just happened to have Kathy and her husband buy a set of plaster cast wall plaques of their babies' hands and feet years ago from Maurice and Mary Jo Garriga, who are part of our fellowship. Some time afterwards they had their little boy's tiny cowboy boot bronzed. Maurice happened to mention to me after I first shared this story about twelve years ago, that he still had the bronzed boot, which he had been unable to deliver because of her arrest and imprisonment. He told me that he'd be happy to have us give it to her if she wanted it. So I dropped her a note.

Kathy was thrilled and sent a letter back right away, "There isn't a thing that the children have left from their childhood. Everything they had was lost, or confiscated somewhere along the line in the series of foster homes that they were in."

The only tangible thing now remaining from their childhood is the bronzed cowboy boot, which God just happened to arrange to have preserved and to allow us to return.

I suspect that the bronzed cowboy boot is probably one of her son's most prized possessions as he now ministers and serves the God who arranged all these details.

THE *OMNIPOTENCE* OF GOD

Jesus told us that the casting out of evil spirits in His name would be the first sign that would follow them that believe (Mk.16:17) and that if He cast out evil spirits by means of the finger of God (Lk.11:20) or the Spirit of God (Mt. 12:28), then without a doubt the kingdom of God had come nigh. So our faith is strengthened today when we perceive the mighty, and powerful deliverances wrought by the hand of God in our day. Just such a dramatic account is that recorded in the next case....

Case 14 "Killer" in Supernatural Strength

The tearful voice of a young woman on the phone said frantically, "I need help, I'm at St. Louis County Hospital right now with my fiance'. One of the nurses gave me your name and said perhaps you could help me with 'Killer' (not his real name). They say here that he is crazy, and they want to lock him up, but he isn't crazy. He thinks he has demons, and I agree."

"What makes you think he has demons?" I replied with my standard response.

"Because he hears voices that tell him to do things he really doesn't want to do. Last night he tried to kill me, and yet he loves me. We're Baptists, and Baptists don't believe in demons, at least at our church they don't. They just say he really needs to get saved again, or re-baptized, and it hasn't helped."

So I invited her to come. When they arrived I learned that Killer had already served time in prison for murder. He was a lean, rather mean looking individual of about 25 wearing blue jeans, a navy pea jacket, and a dark blue wool navy cap. Killer did not really want to come into the store, and didn't seem at all receptive to ministry, which didn't build my faith. He seemed to vacillate between utter rage and an absentminded, almost child-like submissive state. When he shuffled into our prayer room, he looked like one of those individuals you see at a state mental hospital, staring unseeing straight ahead, and being led around by the arm.

Progress was slow, and conversation difficult due to his mood, but I finally learned that Killer had sold himself to Satan at age 12, with a group of older boys, in a rural gang. I was somewhat skeptical, and asked, "*How* did you sell yourself to Satan?"

He replied bluntly, "I drank a blood oath in cat's blood mixed with wine, and recited a ritual."

"Why on earth would you do such a thing?" I inquired

wondering.

"Because I wanted to join the gang, and I wanted the power. I wanted to be strong like they were. I wanted the kind of supernatural strength they had, and *I got it*," he said with obvious pride.

"What kind of powers and supernatural strength did you get?" I asked attempting to conceal my doubt.

"I am *strong!*" he said, and as if reading my mind, he continued, "My hobbies are fighting cops and breaking up church services. (See Mark 1:23) And besides," he continued, "When I go into town, if I see a parking place that I want, and it's already taken, I just get out and lift the other car up on the curb, and park in that space myself."

Needless to say I doubted his story, but a little later while he was in the restroom, I took the opportunity to ask his fiance if it was true, or if she'd ever seen him try it.

"I know it sounds far-fetched, but I've seen it happen lots of times," she confirmed (See Acts 19:13).

In the course of the deliverance, Killer when himself would be meek and submissive, but when the spirits were manifesting themselves through him he would curse and become menacing. He would continually threaten me, and one particular spirit caused him to belligerently point a finger to my nose and keep repeating to me, "I'm going to kill you, Preacher Boy!" This struck me as particularly humorous since I was nearly twice Killer's age, and since I wouldn't have referred to myself as a 'preacher.'

There were several times when Killer became exasperated and would blurt out, "I'm not going to put up with any more of this 'bleep!'" He then would actually get up and walk out of the prayer room. At one point, while standing in the hallway near an all glass exit door, he said to me, "Open this, or else I'll tear it off it's hinges or smash it." He then put his head against the glass, pushing against it like a goat, and I could see the frame beginning to bend under the pressure. Fortunately his girl friend's persuasion prevailed, and he returned to the prayer room.

Another unusual facet of this deliverance illustrates that Satan knows Scripture, and can still quote it when he chooses to. Encountering some challenge made by one of the spirits through Killer, as to my right to intercede for him, I quoted a passage such as Mark 16:17, "These signs shall follow them that believe, in my name they shall cast out devils.." or stated that he was a born again believer, and Christ had died for him. To which the demon mockingly responded in sing-song fashion, "I know all that 'Roman Road' *bleep bleep.*" Then he began to quote again in the same mocking sing-song manner from the Scriptures, such typical Salvation passages as "For all have sinned, and come short of the glory of God;" (Rom. 3:23) and "For whosoever shall call upon the name of the Lord shall be saved." (Rom. 10:9)

We had Killer renounce his oath and covenant with Satan, acknowledge that he wanted to be completely free from it, and ask the Lord to break all such ties. We then came against *witchcraft, murder, hate, drugs, various occult spirits* which he had acquired especially *the occult-power spirit* which had granted him supernatural strength and verbally broke Satan's hold over him.

As the spirits were being cast out, Killer's body straightened, became rigid, his hands pressed down into the pockets of his pea jacket which he had refused to remove. His hands went deeper and deeper into the pockets until there was a loud ripping sound, and both pockets tore loose, and hung down like jagged flaps. Then he grabbed with both hands his wool navy cap, still on his head, and pulled from either side until the top split out of it. Suddenly Killer doubled over with his shoulders touching his knees. Moaning loudly, he grasped the right pant leg of his jeans with both hands and pulled it apart with such strength that the pant leg split to the knee. Then the spirit apparently recognizing that it had lost its battle began to whimper, and whine, and beg to be let alone. It next caused Killer to cower in the corner of the room attempting to hide behind a chair.

As abruptly as this two and a half hour battle had begun, it was over. Killer sat calmly in the chair and smiled rather warmly, until he noticed his clothes and asked incredulously, *"What did you do to me?"*

I could barely suppress a smile as I explained that it was the demon and not I, that had torn his clothing. I then asked, "Killer, are you really saved?"

He said, "I don't think so, now. We've been Baptist, and I've been water-baptized and all the rest, but I really want to accept Him now with all my heart." He turned to his fiance'e and said, "You do, too, don't you?" She nodded in agreement, and I led them in a responsive prayer to accept Jesus as Lord.

As they were leaving, Killer stopped at the door to thank me for helping him. He then turned back to face me again, and said with tears in his eyes, "Brother, if I don't see you again, before, ... I'll see you in heaven."

That really makes this kind of ministry worthwhile.

*** REVELATION: ***
SATAN OR DEMONS CAN IMPART SUPERNATURAL STRENGTH.

*** REVELATION: ***
GOD'S POWER IS GREATER, AND HE PROVIDES HIS PEOPLE SUPERNATURAL PROTECTION.

THE *OMNIPRESENCE* OF GOD:

It has been truly amazing to see the variety of ways God chooses to minister, and the *absolutely limitless power of His ministry.* As an example, I didn't realize how effectively the telephone could be used. Although I shouldn't have been surprised because God is Omnipresent (Everywhere

Present).

One of my first experiences with the use of the telephone in long-distance ministry was with....

Case 15   Dominique in Hawaii

I received a telephone call about ten years ago from a woman whose story demonstrates the *Omnipresence* of God, the fact that God is everywhere, and therefore distance is no barrier at all for Him.

I answered the phone and a French woman identifying herself as Dominique was on the line calling from a telephone booth in Hawaii. She explained, "I want to reach the authors of one of the books which you have published." Then she exploded, "I'm desperate; I'm suicidal!"

"Well, unfortunately," I shared with her, "there is no way to reach those authors; they are out of the country at the moment, but I'd be happy to help you."

She replied, "Oh, thank you, but I need deliverance! I'm suicidal." Her boy friend had deserted her, and she was experiencing rejection and all kinds of problems. "And, in any event," she said, "I'm going to kill myself. I'm going to kill myself *today:* you were my last hope."

"Well," I stalled, "there is still hope, we can pray for you right now."

She said, "Oh, can you pray for me over the phone for deliverance?"

I said, "Sure."

She said, "Oh, that is wonderful. Is that your ministry?"

I thought, "Since it's her dime, and I don't want to get into the whole hassle of trying to explain to her that I have never done this before, and since she is suicidal ... I should at least try to help her." So I responded simply, "Sure."

Thus, knowing that the Lord would forgive me, for trusting Him too much, if I were wrong, I said to her, "Let's just pray."

I had her confess her *unforgiveness, bitterness, hatred* and

106

her feelings of *rejection*. After we dealt with those, I then had her command *the spirit of suicide* to come out of her, and she began to cough and gag.

Visualize the scene: I was sitting at my desk in Kirkwood: nearly half way around the world in Hawaii, in a telephone booth was a woman named Dominique, with a French accent, saying to me, "Oh, Brothaire Beeeel, I feeel so ... seeeck!" I knew the angels must have been rejoicing and laughing at that sight.

I heard from Dominique several more times over the next few months. The Lord had set her free. In fact, she had a number of other people call *for deliverance over the telephone.*

*** REVELATION: ***
GOD'S POWER TO DELIVER IS AVAILABLE EVEN BY TELEPHONE.

God obviously has a great sense of humor, and He's Omniscient (All-Seeing). He's the One that has all the answers. We don't have the answers, and we need to remind ourselves that it is God... It's Jesus who does have the answers and is to be our focus. It reassures us, when we get too wrapped up in the seriousness of other people's problems, that He also has a sense of humor.

Case 16   Adelaide in New Zealand

"Is this the man who was healed of cancer and wrote a book about it?" The voice on the phone inquired. "I'm calling from a local radio station. We just received a call from a woman in New Zealand who has cancer and wants to talk with you. She had called Washington University and asked someone there if they knew you. The person didn't and so referred her for some reason to us. If it's okay with you I'll give her your number when she calls back at 11:00 a.m."

"Sure, that will be fine. Thank you for helping her." I replied, wondering why the lady had chosen to call the university I had attended which was mentioned in the biographical data on the book, instead of calling information for the number of our store or the publishing company.

Precisely at 11:00 a.m. the phone rang and the call was referred to me. "This is Adelaide Jones, calling from New Zealand. Are you Mr. Banks, the man who was healed?"

"Yes," I replied. "And I'm delighted that you finally managed to get through to me."

"Well, I am pretty desperate." She admitted, "I have an inoperable brain tumor, two young daughters and I'm only 29 years old. They have given me no hope, and just two to four months to live. What can I do? I have no hope."

Something in the way she said she had no hope suggested that she didn't have any basis for faith and needed to meet *The Saviour,* as well as *The Healer.* So after sharing some brief faith-building Scriptures and truths concerning healing, I prayed with her for her healing and took authority over the spirits of tumor and cancer, commanding them out of her body. I next asked, "Adelaide, are you saved? Do you know for sure where you'd be right now if you'd been killed in a car accident earlier this morning?"

"No, I really don't." She responded with honesty.

The nape hair on the back of my neck stood on end once again, as I realized what God had arranged: He had a woman in New Zealand who needed Salvation call someone on the opposite side of the world, in order to let her hear the Good News of Jesus's provision for her. I simply explained Salvation to her and then led her in a responsive prayer to accept Jesus. I felt I could almost hear the angels rejoicing with us, and I became aware once again of my insignificance in the whole process. I realized that *I was merely a warm-body, whom God had arranged to have in the right place at the right time to accomplish His purposes.*

*** REVELATION: ***
GOD'S POWER TO SAVE IS ALSO AVAILABLE VIA "LONG DISTANCE."

THE *OMNISCIENCE* OF GOD

God sees all the needs of His people, desires to be their Source and to meet their needs.

Case 17   **Charlie in the Hospital**

Recognition of being a warm-body for God wasn't something new for me, but it is a continually humbling experience. It was extremely humbling the night I realized that God had to almost literally anesthesize me to get me where he wanted me to be.

> "Man's goings are of the Lord; how can a man then understand his own way?"   (Pr. 20:24)

Nearly 16 years ago, I went to Barnes hospital to visit a cancer patient. I shared with him for about five minutes and then his warning that the medication they had given him would "make him sleepy" became reality. I left him sleeping peacefully and decided to make use of the unanticipated free time to try to visit a nurse, Ruth, who had been especially kind to me when I'd been a patient there the year before.

I had been in the hospital on two different occasions spending 45 days on the 10th floor and about 35 on the 5th floor. I got on the elevator and pressed the 10th floor button. When I got off on the 10th floor, however, something was wrong. The carpet didn't seem to be the right pattern, and as I walked down the corridor I noticed the desk area seemed to be on the wrong side of the hallway. I felt as if I were in the midst of a bad dream: everything seemed somehow out of whack. I recognized the black nurse at the desk and asked, "Hi, is Ruth here?"

She looked at me blankly as she responded, "Hi. No we have no one here by that name."

I laughed and said, "Sure, you do. You know Ruth, the cute little blonde nurse who comes in at 3:00 and works a short shift because of her diabetes."

The nurse at the counter shook her head and turned and shouted over her shoulder, "Hey, Mabel, do you know of any nurse here named Ruth, a blonde with diabetes?"

When the other nurses all responded in the negative, I began to think that I had lost my mind. It all seemed like a bad dream. Trying desperately to regain touch with reality, I asked the nurse, "Do you know me?"

She said, "Sure. You're Mr. Banks. You spent a lot of time around the corner in 10005. You were pretty sick, how are you feeling."

I felt pretty stupid about that point, but I shared briefly with her about my healing. Then I began walking back down the corridor toward the elevator still feeling as if I were nuts. Suddenly I heard a voice calling, "Sir. Sir. Excuse me, Sir." Before I could even turn around, I thought to myself, 'She's finally remembered, and I'm not crazy.'

I turned to see a woman coming toward me out of one of the patient's room. She said, "Sir, are you a Minister?"

I answered truthfully to the question she was asking (although I have ministered for 17 years I do not have denominational ordination), "No. I'm not, but can I be of help to you?"

She said, "No, that's okay. I just wanted someone to pray with my husband, and when I saw your Bible, I figured you were a Minister."

"I'm not a Minister, but I'd be happy to pray with your husband."

That apparently satisfied her. She grabbed me by the arm and half-led, half-dragged me to her husband's bedside, where she introduced us, "Sir, this is my husband, Charlie. Charlie, this is some man who'll pray for you." With that out of the way she fled the room leaving Charlie and I there eyeballing one another. I broke the awkward silence, by asking, ''What are you in here for, Charlie?''

He answered by throwing back the covers to reveal his torso which was black and blue from below the neck to the groin, and surgical slits with drain tubes protruding from them. ''Something fell on me at work and crushed me.'' He explained, ''The pain isn't too bad because they've given me pain medication, but my real problem is that I haven't been able to get any sleep in the five days since they've had me here. What I really need is peace, so I can sleep.''

Charlie and I joined hands, rebuked *sleeplessness* and linked our faith as I prayed for the Lord to give him the peace that he desired, as well as the rest and healing which he also needed. I was floating as I left Charlie's room, for I knew that God had answered the prayer spoken that night.

Even though I have never heard from Charlie, and couldn't have, because to him I was just *''some man who'll pray,''* I am convinced that God answered that prayer and gave him peace, rest and healing...because God went to all the trouble of literally anesthesizing me to get me to go to the tenth floor instead of the fifth floor where I'd really intended to go. I did, in fact, go to the fifth floor as soon as I left Charlie's room and found Ruth.

I spent the rest of the evening sharing with her and a group of other nurses who hadn't heard of my healing. They were fascinated by what I'd experienced and asked me to come and share with them again. They said that all they heard about and saw was death and they ''needed to hear more about healings.''

*** REVELATION: ***
IF WE ARE WILLING, GOD CAN USE US IN SPITE OF OURSELVES.

PART SIX

Personal Ministry Teaching Section

I.   Preparing for Your Deliverance
- A.   Make a List of Spirits
- B.   Be Sensitive to the Holy Spirit
- C.   Determine to Be Free

II.   Receiving Your Deliverance
- A.   Be Honest
- B.   Be Teachable
- C.   Be Humble
- D.   Confess and Repent
- E.   Renounce Sins and Satan
- F.   Forgive All Others
- G.   Pray and Take Authority

III.   Keeping Your Deliverance
- A.   Keep Going on With God
- B.   Practice Prayer and Praise
- C.   Stay in Fellowship With Like-Minded Believers
- D.   Study to Become Armed With, and Grounded in the Word
  - 1. The Whole Armour = Jesus!
  - 2. Armour Applied in Maintaining Deliverance
  - 3. 7 Spiritual Warfare Self-Defense Tactics

Personal Ministry Teaching Section

I. PREPARING FOR YOUR DELIVERANCE

Probably the question candidates for deliverance ask most frequently is 'What should I do to prepare myself?' I usually recommend that they read a book on deliverance such as *Songs of Deliverance, Deliver Us From Evil,* or *Pigs in the Parlor,* and something relating to their specific problem area (for example, a woman who's had an abortion should read *Ministering to Abortion's Aftermath).*

Then more specifically, I also recommend the following three preparatory steps:

A. Make a List of Spirits

Prayerfully make a list of the spirits which you feel are bothering you. If you don't know the name, list the characteristics of the spirit or the ways that it manifests itself. This is helpful for you in 'getting a handle' on the spirits you are actually up against. It will serve as a reminder to you once the deliverance session begins, and will assist the one(s) ministering to you in identifying the spirits involved.

B. Be Sensitive to the Holy Spirit

Candidates often ask, "Should I fast?" Again, no hard and fast rules. Sometimes I am led to specifically request it, but most frequently I leave it to the candidate's discretion: "Pray about it, and if you feel you should, by all means do."

C. Determine to Be Free

> "Even so we...were in bondage under the elements of the world: but when the fullness of time was come, God sent forth his Son...made under the law, to redeem them that were under the law, that we might receive the adoption of sons." (Gal. 4:3b-5)
> "If the Son therefore shall make you free, ye shall be free indeed." (John 8:36)

Make a definite decision to get your deliverance! Don't be put off. Satan will attempt to discourage you, to distract you, to make it inconvenient to get the deliverance. Deliverance begins, as do all blessings received from God, with *a decision*. Determine that you want to be free and then having made that decision don't let anything prevent you from obtaining it.

The decision to be free, incorporates the decision to submit oneself to God and to resist the Devil.

> "Submit yourselves therefore to God. Resist the devil, and he will flee from you. Draw nigh to God, and he will draw nigh to you." (James 4:7,8a)
> "Whom resist steadfast in the faith" (I Peter 5:9)

There are several other decisions that the candidate must make....

II. RECEIVING YOUR DELIVERANCE: QUALIFICATIONS FOR, and STEPS TO, DELIVERANCE

I have a friend whose testimony is that he got everything at one time; he was saved, Baptised in the Holy Spirit and instantly delivered of smoking, drinking and cursing. However, most candidates aren't that fortunate, and find that deliverance requires diligence and effort upon their part.

Recognizing that God is sovereign and, of course, can for His purposes grant deliverance at any time, in any place, and to any candidate whom He deems ready, there are still certain qualifications to meet and steps to follow that seem helpful for those desiring deliverance. The following steps are merely offered as guidelines and suggestions. Again, be sensitive to the Holy Spirit: should He tell you to do something not on this list by all means be obedient to His directions.

A. Be Honest

"That we may lead a quiet and peaceable life in all godliness and honesty. For this is good and acceptable in the sight of God our Saviour." (I Tim. 2: 2b-3)

Determine to be totally HONEST, with yourself and with those ministering to you. Don't let the enemy get you to rationalize; admit and face all of your problems. Be willing to renounce all works of darkness in your life; make the decision also to override the resistance of your pride or shame and bring them into the light of God's delivering presence.

Don't waste your time or the time of those ministering to you by being less than totally honest. To not take deliverance seriously can be dangerous, as is to be seen in the accounts in Part Two.

As has been already indicated in some of the cases, a willingness to be totally honest with one's self and with the one(s) assisting you in your deliverance is essential. The Lord has shown us that both fear and demons, like mushrooms thrive in the dark. When we bring the light of God's word and truth to bear upon them they cannot long survive. Be willing to call "sin," sin! Be objective: call your own sin by the same name by which you'd call it in someone else.

B. Be Teachable

Remember that none of us has all the truth. It is therefore important to be willing to be open to God to correct or adjust our theology if it's necessary.

C. Be Humble

"Wherefore he saith, God resisteth the proud, but giveth grace unto the humble." (Jas. 4:6b)
"Humble yourselves therefore under the mighty hand of God, that he may exalt you in due time." (I Pet. 5:6)

Humble yourself by a decision of your will, and willfully do battle with your pride, or your desire for dignity, if it comes to that. Determine to choose to be free and to have your deliverance, rather than your dignity. Recognizing that it is only Satan who would tell you that your dignity is in jeopardy.

D. Confess and Repent

"Confess your faults one to another..." (Jas. 5:16a)
"And many that believed came, and confessed, and shewed their deeds.." (Acts 19:18)

It is important for the candidate to confess any known sins (especially those which relate to the business at hand), and to repent of that sinful behavior. If the candidate is unwilling to call adultery, "adultery," or fornication, "fornication," then the one ministering will need to point out that that's what it is. Naming a sin by its Scriptural name is helpful for the candidate to recognize his sin for what it truly is in God's eyes, and to be able to properly identify and confess it as the sin that it is.

E. Renounce Sins and Satan

"But have renounced the hidden things of dishonesty, not walking in craftiness..." (2 Cor.4:2)

To renounce is to give up all right or claim to something; usually by a formal public statement. It also means to cast off, to disown; to refuse to further associate with; and to repudiate all ties. Specifically here it means to sever all ties with sin, Satan's kingdom and any unrighteousness.

F. Forgive All Others

"And when ye stand praying, forgive, if ye have aught against any, that your Father also which is in heaven may forgive you..." (Mk. 11:25)

Forgiveness has played an essential part in more than 90% of the deliverances which we have ministered over the last 17 years. One should become familiar with the steps to forgiveness in the Forgiveness Teaching Section in Part Seven. The candidate should pray a simple prayer forgiving all who are felt to have wronged him, such as the following:

"Lord Jesus, I come to you confessing my unforgiveness as sin. I renounce all sins involved in my harboring unforgiveness against _____ and _____ . I give up my right to be angry with them, and now, by a decision of my will I forgive them for wronging me, and I ask you to forgive them as well. Amen.

G. Pray and Take Authority

"I will pray with the Spirit, and I will pray with the understanding also..." (I Cor. 14:15)

Determine like Paul to Pray with the Spirit and with your understanding (in your native language) also. Each day one must make the decision to pray in English or one doesn't pray in English; the same decision must be made to pray in the Spirit. The blessings and benefits of each can only flow when prayer is utilized. As you pray ask God to reveal to you any areas of darkness that remain within you which need to be dealt with.

Finally, USE YOUR AUTHORITY.

"And these signs shall follow them that believe; in my name shall they cast out devils.." (Mk. 16:17a)

God has invested you with unbelievable power and authority. You are a *believer*, the power is yours! Having done the previous steps, now use the authority given to you

119

and the privilege of invoking the Name of Jesus — command each spirit, by name, to leave you right now in Jesus' Name!

> *In the name of Jesus Christ, I take authority over the spirit(s) tormenting me. I bind you, you spirit of _____ , and I command you to leave me right now in Jesus' name!*

NOTE: During the actual deliverance, if someone else is ministering to you: don't pray in the Spirit, or use Jesus' name after the initial command, while the evil spirits are being cast out. For the power entailed in each of these Spiritual weapons often causes the spirits to draw back and attempt to hide, rather than come out.

III. KEEPING YOUR DELIVERANCE

Deliverance Must Be Maintained: Seven Important Keys

Having for more than 16 years held weekly healing services, a certain characteristic of human nature has become obvious to us. People tend 'to want what they want, when they want it,' and once they have what they want from God, the vast majority are content to return to their old way of life. God's prophet, Isaiah, said that there would be a great forsaking of God by His people, but that there would be a faithful remnant of 10%. God's figure of 10% is probably pretty accurate in so far as the 1000's we've prayed for go: few seem to want more of God than just what's needed to have their immediate needs met. The desire of the majority is not sufficient to cause them to continue seeking God after the immediate need is met.

Many have come, received great blessings of healing, Salvation, Baptism in the Spirit, or deliverance from the hand of the Lord and then we never see them again. They go back to their dead churches, or some slightly more alive fellowships, and we don't see them, until a new need arises. There are certain people whom we know have a sickness or need in the family, if they show up at our meetings.

120

When sick or in need they return: when they don't, they don't. The same principle holds true to a certain degree with regard to deliverance, there are several very important steps to maintaining deliverance.

These comments are not intended to in any way lift up our meetings as spiritually superior to any other, but rather to sound a warning. We've seen that unless delivered individuals seek like-minded fellowship and Bible teaching which can stimulate them, all too often they cease both to grow and to go on with God.

A. Keep Going on With God

We can only reasonably expect our car's battery to remain charged if we run the car to charge it. By the same token, we need to continue seeking God in order to keep our spiritual batteries charged. Stay close to your Source; for where your heart is, there your treasure will be also. The blessings of God are to be found with God.

Keep seeking God: remain open to Him. Never make the fatal assumption, that you 'have arrived,' 'have it all,' or don't need more. If one mistakenly believes that, then there is an automatic cessation of seeking God for more. No man, with the exception of Jesus, has ever even come close to receiving all that God has for him.

B. Practice Prayer and Praise

People often ask me, as a former, terminal cancer patient, if I see my doctor regularly. I reply, "No, but I stay in daily contact with the One who healed me!" God has healed or delivered you for a purpose to *have fellowship with Him and to share Him with others.* He desires a relationship with you. A Christian is a (Spiritual) tree of the Lord's planting (Isa. 61:3) and definitely needs a life of prayer and praise just as a natural tree needs water and sunlight to prosper.

121

C. Stay in Fellowship With Like-Minded Believers

If one doesn't associate with Believers who are at least as mature or as advanced as he is, and preferable some who are even more mature, he won't grow. If an adult associates only with children — he is living but he isn't going to be intellectually stimulated. So it is with those who are past the milk stage in their walk, if one chooses to remain in a spiritual kindergarten with babes.. one will remain a child. One must feed himself with the Word and with mature spiritual fellowship.

Also it is important to use and share what you have received. James states this Scriptural principle of 'getting and giving,' when he tells us to "pray one for another that we may be healed." It holds true with healing and it holds true of deliverance and spiritual health. We need like-minded fellowship for growth, encouragement and ministry.

D. Study to Become Armed With, and Grounded in the Word

Endeavor to read the word daily, and especially familiarize yourself with the whole armour of God as described in Ephesians. The Lord gave me a revelation years ago concerning the whole armour:

1. The Whole Armour = Jesus!

Early in 1972 the Lord gave me an understanding concerning the "whole Armour of God" mentioned in Chapter six of Ephesians. Recently, more than a dozen years later He has shown me another confirmation of that truth and a specific Scriptural statement of its accuracy.

The Scripture concerned is:

"Finally, my brethren, be strong in the Lord, and in the power of His might.

"Put on the whole armour of God, that ye may be able

to stand against the wiles of the devil.

"For we wrestle not against flesh and blood, but against principalities, against powers, against the rulers of the darkness of this world, against spiritual wickedness in high places.

"Wherefore take unto you the whole armour of God, that ye may be able to withstand in the evil day, and having done all, to stand.

"Stand therefore, having your loins girt about with truth, and having on the breastplate of righteousness;

"And your feet shod with the preparation of the gospel of peace;

"Above all, taking the shield of faith, wherewith ye shall be able to quench all the fiery darts of the wicked.

"And take the helmet of salvation, and the sword of the Spirit, which is the word of God:

"Praying always with all prayer and supplication in the Spirit." (Eph.6:10-18)

What is the **whole armour of God?** Permit me to show you with a series of questions.

"Stand therefore having your loins girt about with **truth**"

Who said, "I am the way, the **truth**, and the life!"

"And having on the breastplate of **righteousness;**"

Who is the source of our **righteousness?** Who is, Himself, the **righteousness** of God?

"And your feet shod with the preparation of the gospel of **peace;**"

Who is the Prince of **Peace?** In celebration of whose birth did the angels sing, **"Peace** on earth!"?

"Above all, taking the shield of **faith,** wherewith ye shall be able to quench all the fiery darts of the wicked."

Who is it who is the Author and Finisher of our **faith?**

"And take the helmet of **salvation,**"

Who is the source of our **Salvation?** Whose very name, *YESHUA,* means **Salvation?**

"And the sword of the Spirit, which is **the word of God:**"

Who is known as **the Word of God** and also was the **Word made flesh?** Who...the very Logos of God?

"Praying always with all prayer and supplication **in the Spirit,**"

Who is it that baptises us with the Holy Spirit and thereby enables us to pray **in the Spirit**"?

Thus, I feel it is clear that it is Jesus that is every element of the armour, and therefore, is Himself the **whole armour of God;** the very fullness of the Godhead, being all in all. He is our Leader, Captain, King, and even our **Armour** — our source of protection. He provides (as Jehovah-Jireh) for our every need and here the need provided for is that of our protection against the wiles and weapons of our malignant enemy.

Jesus has given us other equipping — the legal right to another weapon, **His Name**...before which every knee must ultimately bow. He has also given us power! There are two different words in the Greek translated as "power" in the New Testament, and Jesus has provided us both forms of power: *exousia* — the legal right, or *authority,* and *dunamis* — the dynamite *enabling power* to do "greater works" than He Himself had done because He has won the right to pour forth the Spirit upon all willing flesh!

You will recall that I said the Lord had reconfirmed the validity of this revelation over a dozen years later. He did that also with His Word in Romans 13:12,14 another reference to the Armour of God:

"The night is far spent, the day is at hand: let us therefore cast off the works of darkness, and let us put on the armour of light.
"But put ye on **the Lord Jesus Christ** and make not provision for the flesh, to fulfill the lusts thereof."

Here the Lord is telling us to dispel the works of darkness — the works of Satan's kingdom, by means of bringing the light of the Word of God, the light of the Gospel, the light of Jesus and the illumination of His Holy Spirit, to bear upon them. He also plainly states that rather than being a party to those works of darkness, we are to make ourselves separate from them and to defend ourselves by means of *the armour of light*...**by putting on "the Lord Jesus Christ"**! To put on Jesus Christ *is* to put on the whole armour of God!

As beautiful as what I feel He has shown me is, I can see that He still has even more, varied depths of truth here. Any truth about Jesus can be substituted into our formula to represent the elements of the armour. For example, Jesus is the Word of God. Therefore we can truthfully say that the Word of God is also defensive **truth,** and provides righteousness, peace, faith, Salvation and is, of course, correctly called the sword of the Spirit — the Word of God.

2. *Armour Applied in Maintaining Deliverance*

The Helmet of Salvation is especially important in guarding your mind from every assault, and from questioning your Salvation. But it is also effective against Satan's primary area of attack, the thought life. Gird up the loins of your mind to utilize the helmet. Just as we would repel an attack against our Salvation by employing the Word, "I am saved because it is written..." An expression of our faith is a positive confession, not attempting to claim something, but positively confessing a good confession, stating about ourselves what the Word of God has said concerning us. We also make a positive confession, not because we're superstitiously afraid of saying something negative, like 'knocking on wood.' Rather, we need to come to the point of recognizing that we are speaking from our position of safety under the helmet, and that our minds are protected.

> ### 7 Spiritual Warfare Self-Defense Tactics
>
> 1 Applying the blood to the door posts of your mind.
> 2 Putting your mind under the blood.
> 3 Quoting Scriptures to refute Satan, and to build up your own faith.
> 4 Mentally refusing to listen to Satan's lies; simply tune him out.
> 5 Praying and especially Praying in the Spirit. (Satan and demons hate tongues.)
> 6 Acknowledge that Jesus is your defense, and that Satan has to get through Jesus to come at you.
> 7 When Satan attacks with a doubt, fear, or temptation, use that as a reminder to counterattack him with Prayer, Praying in the Spirit or by employing one of the other Tactics.

E. Walk Out Your Deliverance

Continue to make the decision daily until it ceases to be necessary, to not fall back into the area of temptation. Recall that although demons can indeed be cast out by believers, believers are also instructed that the *flesh must be crucified*.

I normally tell people who have been delivered, "God has done the supernatural part of this deliverance. Now you must do the natural part: you must make the decision not to go back into your old patterns of sinning."

An important related area that is often overlooked is that of

*** HABITS ***

The old habits, fleshly appetites, lusts and desires, have to go. We may find it necessary to discipline ourselves to cease indulging our flesh, but such self-discipline will yield good fruit.

If you were delivered from alcoholism, you must recognize that although God has sovereignly delivered you, (that is, He has broken the supernatural bondage to alcohol) there may still be *habit patterns* to be broken. If, for example, it was your custom every afternoon at 3:00 to meet your friends at the local bar — then you will have to make the decision not to go to the bar at 3:00. God will not make that decision for you, or else you'd be merely a robot. You still have free-will even after you've been delivered. You can go to the tavern or not go, but if you do go you will probably wind up soon forfeiting your deliverance.

Another situation is that which involves harlotry or adultery. If you have been set free from this kind of lust, then you will need to avoid any individual who would draw you back into that type of sin no matter how much you may care for him or her. This "loved one" becomes the worst enemy of your soul, and your spiritual freedom as well as your life is at stake.

God is not an "Indian-giver." He will not take back what He's given to you ("For the gifts and calling of God are without recall." Rom.11:29), but the enemy is no gentleman and he will steal your deliverance if given half a chance. If you go back to the bar, you are going back onto his turf...he will probably have someone bait you with an argument like this, "If you're really free, you should be able to go in there and witness to your old friends, or at least be able to turn down a drink — *if* you're *really* free." This is the same kind of ploy which he used unsuccessfully on Jesus in the wilderness, "If you are the Son of God...' then test it, or prove it by..."

Satan is a robber and will give the illusion of having stolen your deliverance if you let him convince you that you don't have it (didn't really get it), that he has stolen it, or that you have somehow lost it. In actual fact, Satan and all the demons in Hell aren't powerful enough to take away from you what Jesus Christ has given to you. This is true of the Baptism of the Holy Spirit and the prayer language that comes with it, and it is equally true of deliverance. We can only lose what God has given us by a.) refusing to believe that He has done it for us, b.) by ceasing to use what he's given (by not walking in it), or c.) by surrendering to Satan through choosing to return to our old ways and by not 'going on with God.'

F. Change Your Attitudes

On the surface this may seem impossible, but God is in the business of changing man for the better. We cooperate with Him, by making the decision to obey Phil. 4:8, "Finally, brethren, whatsoever things are true ... honest ... just ... pure ... lovely ... of good report; if there be any virtue, and if there be any praise, *think on these things.* "

Simply put: We, prayerfully with God's assistance, determine to look for good, rather than evil, in persons, places and situations.

G. Crucify the Flesh and Commit Self Totally to Christ

If a temptation reoccurs, resist it immediately. If an attempt to return is made by a spirit, cast it out immediately. Do not entertain an unwanted guest: cast it out yourself, or get assistance from other believers. For some who've been deeply bound, it may be that daily deliverance will be required until you're totally free.

> "For if while we were enemies we were reconciled to God through the death of His Son, it is much more [certain], now that we are reconciled, that we shall be saved *[daily delivered* from sin's dominion] through His [resurrection] life."   (Rom. 8:10 Amplif. Bible)

A final closing thought in reference to maintaining deliverance: Remember, we can set our will against the sin of doubt, just as we would set our will against any other sin. As we stand firm against the doubt, the Holy Spirit will come to our assistance and strengthen our faith.

* * * * * * *

PART SEVEN

Epilogue

Epilogue

A. GOD'S MESSAGE FOR THIS HOUR!!

In this hour God is telling His Body, the church, that she must grow up! She must become mature and prepared for spiritual warfare!

> "Behold, I send you forth as sheep in the midst of wolves: be ye therefore wise as serpents, and harmless as doves." (Mt. 10:16)

God wants His people prepared also to be delivered from the world, the flesh and the Devil.

This is the beginning of His time to complete His purpose of preparing a Bride for Himself...a Bride who is to be without spot, wrinkle or other blemish. A beloved Bride who is to be perfected by Him, "That He might sanctify and cleanse" her "with the washing of water by the word."

God by means of His Word is going to wash and cleanse this Bride from all uncleanness, and purify her from every work of darkness or any link with Satan's realm. He is restoring to His Body the truths concerning deliverance in this hour, that His people might be set free from every taint of sin that has so easily beset us, in order that we might truly become that glorious Bride and that victorious, Mighty Army of fully equipped Christian Soldiers who will go forth in His power and enabling, to defeat all the hosts of Hell and cast down her very gates!

God gave a word, "Be aware...Be Wary...BeWare!" What did this mean? He is warning us once again against the potential of 5th column activity within our very midst:

133

"For such are **false Apostles,** deceitful workers, transforming themselves into the **apostles of Christ.**

"And no marvel; for Satan himself is transformed into **an angel of light.** Therefore it is no great thing if his ministers also be transformed as the **ministers of righteousness;** whose end shall be according to their works."

God is warning us that we must be on Guard, that we must become mature and grow up. He is warning us that all who profess to be believers and to be "of God" may not be "walking in the Light." Therefore, it is incumbent upon us to "test and try the spirits," and exercise spiritual discernment. We must be willing to see error, no matter how painful such seeing may be for us. We would prefer to see only good...but the Word tells us that "those who by reason **of use** have their senses exercised to discern **both good and evil"** *will see both!* (Heb. 5:14b) Paul continues the same type of admonition when he states, "But he that is spiritual **judgeth all things."**

Paul clearly tells us that if we are to be spiritual, we must exercise spiritual discernment in all areas concerning the things of the Kingdom. Therefore, be wary of any minister who says to you, "Don't judge me! Don't judge my ministry." That man is wrong, and is giving unscriptural advice. You and I must judge... we must discern. You should be praying for discernment right now, even as you read this material; is it valid, is it of God, does it align with the Word of God or is it error? You must ask yourself these kinds of questions or you may find yourself being misled as so many have, into following cultish leaders. The followers of Jim Jones and other such men, obviously didn't prayerfully check their doctrines, teachings, and ministries against the word of God and against simple common sense! God does not tell people to put their brains in a sack and throw them away when they become Christians. He instead encourages us to be both wise and discerning!!

The church is in trouble today for several reasons: first it has not been open to, nor given proper honor to the Holy Spirit. It has also been too rigid, too doctrine-conscious, and too insufficiently God-conscious.

A prophetic warning which we have heard given several times concerning various pastors or their churches could be paraphrased or summarized as:

> **You have become like mighty trees, like mighty oaks, in the branches of which the birds have come to find shelter, comfort and to build their nests; but you have become too rigid and you cannot bend with the breeze... only a great storm, like a hurricane could move you. I choose to come as a gentle breeze.**

God apparently desires His people, the "trees of his planting," to be flexible, yielded to, and sensitive to the moving of His Spirit, as was indicated in a vision described on another occasion in a different segment of His Body:

> **"I saw a cluster of trees on the top of a hill or cliff. The wind came and blew, and the trees bent (bowed) over almost touching the ground, and then as the wind passed by, the trees sprang back into their upright position."**

God, I feel, desires a people who can and will be sensitive to His Spirit. He is not seeking rigidity, or inflexibility but rather sensitivity to his Spirit.

B. A CHALLENGE TO BELIEVERS

You have received authority *(exousia)* with your Salvation, and you have also received power *(dunamis)* with the Baptism in the Holy Spirit. It is quite possible that you do not yet fully realize the significance and extent of the authority and power which have been conveyed unto you. I would therefore encourage you to seek God for a fuller understanding. I'll issue you the same challenge which I myself received more than 17 years ago expressed in the following statements:

> "I *am everything* that Jesus Christ
>   says that I am.
> I *can do everything* that Jesus Christ
>   says that I can do."

I now challenge you to delve into the Word of God and find out just exactly whom *Jesus Christ says that you are* and just what *Jesus Christ says that you, in the power of His name, can do.*

Index of Evil Spirits Encountered

IMPACT CHRISTIAN BOOKS, INC.

Announces

SONGS OF DELIVERANCE

BILL BANKS

FOREWORD BY GLENN G. DUDLEY, M.D.

The Exciting New Power for Deliverance Series:

Power for Deliverance; Songs of Deliverance
Power for Deliverance From Fat
Power for Deliverance for Children
Power for Deliverance From Childlessness

Lives have already been changed by the powerful truths and revelations contained in these books as the author has taught them over the past seventeen years. These deliverance tools have been tested in the crucible of prayer room battles to free lives from Satan's control. You have tasted in this book the kind of dramatic accounts and truths which are to be found in the other volumes in this series.

Each book is just $5.95. When ordering, add $1.50 postage and handling for the first book and $.50 for each additional title.

Available at your local Christian bookstore, library,
or directly from:

Impact Christian Books, Inc.
332 Leffingwell Avenue, Suite 101
Kirkwood, MO 63122

DELIVERANCE FOR CHILDREN & TEENS

The first Practical Handbook for Ministering Deliverance to Children.

The material in this book is arranged to help parents in diagnosing their children's problems and in finding solutions for destructive behavior patterns.

The **Doorways** Section of this book illustrates how demons enter, and how they take advantage of innocent, vulnerable children. More than a dozen categories of routes of entry are identified, and examples given!

The section on **Discipline** will be especially helpful to parents who wish to avoid problems, or remove them before they can become entrenched.

The **Mechanics of Ministry** Section will help you, step by step, in ministering to a child needing help.

You will learn simple, surprising truths. For example...
✿ Easiest of all ministry is to small children! ✿ Discipline is the most basic form of Spiritual Warfare and can bring deliverance! ✿ A child can acquire demonic problems through Heredity or Personal Experience! ✿ Deliverance need not be frightening if properly presented!

$6.95, Plus $1.00 Shipping

IMPACT CHRISTIAN BOOKS, INC.
332 Leffingwell Ave., Suite 101
Kirkwood, MO 63122

Are you aware that demonic spirits can prevent childbirth?

DELIVERANCE FROM CHILDLESSNESS

During the first year this book was in print eight babies were conceived by women formerly diagnosed as "incapable of having children!"

This book offers the first real hope for certain childless couples...because, for some, there is a **spiritual** rather than a physical block preventing conception.

The testimonies included will build your faith as will the Scriptural truths revealed. Surprisingly the Scripture says quite a bit about childlessness and gives:
    * reports of at least 9 unexpected or miraculous births granted to formerly childless or barren mothers;
    * examples of women who were healed of barrenness;
    * children granted in answer to prayer;
    * instances of children denied because of *a curse of childlessness*

You will also learn:
    * How curses of childlessness come into being, and how they may be broken.
    * Ways that spirits of infertility and sterility enter, and how to cast them out.

THE HEAVENS DECLARE . . .

William D. Banks

More than 250 pages!
More than 50 illustrations!

- Who named the stars and why?
- What were the original names of the stars?
- What is the secret message hidden in the stars?

The surprising, **secret message** contained in the earliest, original names of the stars, is revealed in this new book.

The deciphering of the star names provides a fresh revelation from the heart of **the intelligence** behind creation. Ten years of research includes material from the British Museum dating prior to 2700 B.C.

A clear explanation is given showing that early man had a sophisticated knowledge of One, True God!

$6.95 + $1.50 Shipping/Handling

ALIVE AGAIN!

William D. Banks

The author, healed over twelve years ago, relates his own story. His own testimony presents a miracle or really a series of miracles — as seen through the eyes of a doubting skeptic, who himself becomes the object of the greatest miracle, because he is Alive Again!

The way this family pursues and finds divine healing as well as a great spiritual blessing provides a story that will at once bless you, refresh you, restore your faith or challenge it! You will not be the same after you have read this true account of the healing gospel of Jesus Christ, and how He is working in the world today.

The healing message contained in this book needs to be heard by every cancer patient, every seriously ill person, and by every Christian hungering for the reality of God.

More than a powerful testimony — here is teaching which can introduce you or those whom you love to healing and to a new life in the Spirit!

$4.95 + $1.50 Shipping/Handling

Impac Christian Books

332 Leffingwell Ave., Suite 101
Kirkwood, MO 63122

AVAILABLE AT YOUR LOCAL BOOKSTORE, OR YOU MAY
ORDER DIRECTLY. Toll-Free, order-line only M/C, DISC,
or VISA 1-800-451-2708.

Write for *FREE* Catalog.